# CULTŪRA

A GUIDEBOOK TO HELP FOUNDERS
DESIGN ORGANIZATIONAL CULTURES
FOR DIVERSE TEAMS

## MICHEL FABODE

MANUSCRIPTS
**PRESS**



CULTŪRA

*A guidebook to help founders design organizational cultures for diverse teams*

ISBN        979-8-88926-542-9  *Paperback*

979-8-88926-543-6  *Ebook*

*To the community of family (by blood
and by love), friends, church life group,
educators, business leaders, and many others
who have poured into me throughout the
years—I have learned everything I know
about building culture from you. Thank
you for being such exquisite teachers.*

# CONTENTS

———

# INTRODUCTION

How often do you think about culture?

I suspect it's probably as often as you think about air. Both are omnipresent, yet you cannot buy a bottle of either. There are, however, those moments when they come to the forefront of our senses, typically because we have experienced something surprising, whether positive or negative.

I am a marketer and former marketing professor turned culture and organizational development consultant, and I relish the opportunities I get to help leaders in early-stage operations build high-performing organizations for truly diverse teams.

These leaders understand the importance and value of building teams of people from varying backgrounds and perspectives. They do not need a business case for diversity as they are already fully bought into the innovative power of teams with as many dimensions of diversity as the talent pool will enable (e.g., diverse backgrounds, experiences, racial and ethnic groups, gender identities, nationalities, etc.).

Having strong convictions about building diverse, innovative teams and actually *doing this* are two different things.

There are several commonly cited reasons as to why, ranging from a lack of diverse applicants to the idea that, particularly in the early stages of building an organization, leaders have to worry more about keeping the lights on as opposed to who's flipping the switches. I will contend that there is a far more common reason that leaders can often struggle with building and supporting teams that align with their convictions.

> "Having strong convictions about building diverse, innovative teams and actually doing this are two different things."

To explain, let's talk about water.

Everyone on Earth needs water, and no matter what, every drop of substance labeled "water" is based on the same formula: two atoms of hydrogen and one of oxygen. If you go to the grocery store to buy water, you will find a wide variety of options in a shocking range of prices. Some have electrolytes, others have sweeteners, and others are packaged in cardboard rather than plastic.

Why? Each of these water brands is targeting customers who, they hope, will buy their water product to meet a specific need (e.g., "I need water with electrolytes after an intense workout," or "I need to drink water with some flavor") or align with a specific belief (e.g., "I should use less plastic, so I want my water in a cardboard container"). As such, each brand has made decisions about packaging and taste with these customer needs in mind.

In my observations, most leaders will tend to behave like our water brand managers above when building their organizations, crafting the organization to meet the needs of target customers. In many cases, however, the target customer is the leader.

According to *First Round Review*, a blog created by the venture firm First Round Capital, 80 percent of a company's culture is a reflection of its core leaders (*First Round Review* 2014). It is no wonder we can often learn a lot about an organization simply by studying the composition of its leaders and the behaviors that are promoted and rewarded within its structure.

The result of this inclination to build organizations that reflect themselves is that, despite the best of intentions, leaders can often find themselves with shockingly homogeneous teams. When this happens, these leaders can struggle to cultivate innovation in the organization and attract more diverse perspectives. But as our demographics shift, the challenges here will not stop there.

The eldest members of Gen Z, those born after 1996, are now beginning to enter the workforce, and as it turns out, this generation is the most diverse one the US has ever seen (Parker and Igielnik 2020). So, an inability to intentionally build diverse teams at *all* levels of the organization may soon make accessing human capital the primary business risk facing these leaders.

The good news is that all is not lost, and leaders committed to building diverse teams can absolutely do so in a manner that maximizes innovation and supercharges their business strategy. To do this, though, they must embrace two things: the mindset of a 15° Founder and the toolkit of a culture designer.

The 15° Founders are a collection of leaders insistent on building organizations with diverse individuals to solve a particular problem. These leaders may be at the helm of organizations from small businesses to Fortune 500s, tech startups to non-profits, hospitals to schools, and everything in between. What distinguishes them is how intentional they are about building teams of people with truly diverse backgrounds and perspectives and who are united by the organization's mission.

Notably, though, 15° Founders are also distinguished by their willingness to take inventory of who they are and who they are not in order to thoughtfully construct teams that can help minimize their blind spots and execute beyond their individual capacity. Just as driving experts recommend adjusting the side mirrors by about fifteen degrees to eliminate the blind spot and expand the driver's field of view, 15° Founders recognize that building organizations to solve real problems requires people fundamentally different from themselves to expand their business field of view (NHTSA 2011).

As the workforce becomes increasingly diverse, 15° Founders will be positioned to recruit and retain the best workers, particularly if they can intentionally design a culture for a diverse team. Harnessing the power of a passionate and diverse team requires the culture design toolkit. This toolkit can give 15° Founders the mechanisms for thoughtfully and intentionally crafting a culture for that team.

Without the right culture, even teams optimized for diversity give in to conformity, thereby minimizing the value of the team's diverse perspectives and becoming its own kryptonite. Too often, 15° Founders do not have meaningful guidance for how to create a culture that guards against this and fosters the specific values that drive success.

This book is that guide.

Throughout this book, I will discuss the characteristics of a 15° Founder and provide frameworks and real examples to help you design a culture for diverse teams that maximizes business performance.

I have had the unique experience of working for companies ranging from startups to Fortune 500s and across healthcare, tech, and advisory services. Over the course of my career, I've developed a passion for applying marketing principles in the talent space and a healthy obsession with what it takes to cultivate belonging. I've also had the opportunity to closely engage with a number of tech startup founders.

The frameworks and examples of culture design I share in this book will be illustrated by these experiences and more, including lessons from a Fortune 500 executive, insights from cult classic movies, and wisdom gleaned from a price hike at my son's daycare.

Leaders who read this book will gain clarity on:

1. The importance of linking the customer experience to the employee experience;
2. How insights gained from self-awareness are crucial to informing the culture you want to create; and
3. Why sincerity must thoughtfully underpin your culture.

As a bonus, you'll learn how to think and act like a 15° Founder.

Are you ready?

## CHAPTER 1

# WHO ARE YOU AS A FOUNDER?

———

Congratulations! You're invited to be a judge on a new reality competition show, *Top Host*.

*Top Host* is the first televised competition for the country's most extraordinary dinner party hosts. Hosts will compete for the title of Top Host and a chance to win a million dollars. The finale will feature the top two contestants competing head-to-head by hosting a three-course dinner for one of two possible guest lists.

Guest list one consists of five James Beard Award-winning chefs. Guest list two also consists of five individuals, but they are each very different: a seventeen-year-old entrepreneur, a retired three-star general, a TikTok influencer, a mechanical engineer, and your most eccentric cousin. As a judge, you will be responsible for assessing whether the two finalists create thoughtful, memorable experiences for their guests. You must answer: Which host is best poised to win the million dollar prize?

As you can imagine, much of that depends on the skills of the two finalists. However, as a judge in this hypothetical competition, you must recognize the two guest lists will test them in different ways.

Creating a dining experience for the first list requires the ability to impress five individuals who have mastered their craft and made careers out of creating experiences around food. These five individuals are likely to have some things in common regarding what they expect from a well-designed dining experience.

Creating the experience for the second list, however, will test the finalist's ability to consider each guest's individual needs. The diverse composition of this guest list means the host will not be able to anchor themselves on one given standard for what a good dining experience should be. Instead, they will need to craft an experience that delights each of these five very different people. As you may have surmised, the finalists who are hosting these two guest lists are not actually playing the same game.

While *Top Host* is hypothetical (for now, at least), this scenario is akin to what we see daily in the business world. Too often, leaders of organizations large and small, from non-profits to for-profits, genuinely desire to build organizations comprised of people as bombastically different as those on guest list two. They want to unlock the innovative potential that comes with truly diverse teams. Yet, they approach the task without recognizing that creating an optimal experience for guest list two will require a very different approach than guest list one.

It must also be noted that the experience designed for a diverse group of individuals will be materially different from one for a less diverse group. One need only imagine the difference between dining with a group of James Beard Award winners and dining with a seemingly random assortment of people. Undoubtedly, the nature of the conversations and the independent perceptions will differ wildly.

One scenario is more likely to feature commentary on the texture of the food and whether or not certain flavors clashed. In contrast, the other is more likely to feature some combination of foreign diplomatic relations and the latest TikTok challenges. In the business world and throughout this book, I will describe that difference as a function of culture.

According to *Merriam-Webster*, "culture" is the shared attitudes, values, goals, and practices that characterize an institution or organization (Merriam-Webster 2023). I have always been fascinated by the pervasiveness of culture in literally any setting. In the business world, it shows up in what's seen and what isn't, at times driving a team to go above and beyond to get a job done, at others implicitly giving a team permission to do the bare minimum to address a need. It is no wonder leaders often quote the adage, "Culture eats strategy for lunch."

> Culture is shaped at the top of an organization, and this shaping happens whether the leaders know they are doing it or not.

One thing many of us often overlook about culture is the fact that it is not random. While leaders are not always intentional about crafting the culture in many settings, the culture itself is rarely inexplicable. According to *First Round Review*, a blog created by the venture firm First Round Capital, 80 percent of a company's culture is defined by the core leaders of an organization (*First Round Review* 2014). This means the shared attitudes, values, and practices of an organization's leaders have an outsized impact on its cultural norms.

Sit with that for a minute.

I have found that I can trace an organization's critical cultural traits directly to the characteristics of its leaders. Why? Because culture is shaped at the top of an organization, and this shaping happens whether the leaders know they are doing it or not.

So, if culture eats strategy for lunch, and culture is shaped at the top of an organization, one would assume that leaders—particularly new founders—would give due consideration to their cultures from the very inception of the organization itself. However, this tends to differ from the conventional wisdom.

According to Crunchbase, the first five priorities for every startup founder should be (Cole 2018):

- Cash
- Building a sales machine
- Building the founder's thought leader brand
- Learning from early customers
- Making self-care a habit

Similarly, according to an *Entrepreneur* article, the top challenges founders need to address are cash flow, marketing and advertising, transparency, burning out, and leaving "DEI initiatives for established organizations" (Longgrear 2023). Conventional wisdom clearly does not make organizational culture a priority.

I had a discussion on this topic with Tawana Rivers, a thirty-year human resources professional—plus cofounder and chief executive officer of The 10K Project, which aims to drive economic empowerment within the black community by pairing black founders with black investors. This means Rivers engages with many black entrepreneurs in the earliest stages of building their businesses.

According to Rivers, culture is typically not prioritized at this phase because these entrepreneurs are in survival mode. For black founders, this is particularly true: according to Crunchbase, they received only 1.2 percent of total venture capital invested in US startups during the first half of 2021—and that was double the 2020 investment figures (Van Romburgh and Teare 2021).

Rivers adds that founders must "think about [culture] before [they're] ready to execute on it." Otherwise, she believes founders risk facing many issues we see in later-stage organizations that failed to be thoughtful at their inception.

Leaders, particularly founders, who are intentional about their organizational culture right from the start optimize their long-term chances of success. Given a founder's role in the culture itself, being deliberate from day one is a matter of owning who you are as a leader and, consequently, who you will be as an organization. Put differently, thoughtfulness around culture enables you to articulate who you are as a Top Host and which guests will have a positive experience at your dinner party.

There is an ever-growing group of business leaders aspiring to be *Top Host* equivalents with the skills to successfully design cultures for teams as diverse as guest list two. For some, the driving force here may be that they have had personal experiences with poorly designed or non-inclusive organizational cultures. For others, it may be recognition that shifting demographics in the US will give leaders who can build and lead truly diverse teams a competitive edge.

Either way, with the guidance in the following pages, these leaders will be well-positioned to design cultures that can optimize their business for success by attracting and retaining diverse talent. When I refer to diverse talent, I refer to the identities that most often define our lived experiences, including race, ethnicity, gender identity, nationality, sexual orientation, etc.

## Special note

Throughout this book, I will refer to the leaders committed to building and directing diverse teams as "founders." I do this for simplicity as it pertains to who is defining an organization's culture. In many cases, the organization's current leaders will not be its founders. The concepts I explain still apply. However, when the founder *is* still in the leadership seat, that person's thoughtfulness about culture will have an impact that can well outlast their tenure at the helm. They will be able to embed traits into the culture that can, often, only be undone with radical and transformational changes to the organization.

Organizational cultures that have been optimized for the contributions of diverse individuals, unfortunately, do not happen by accident. Instead, they result from very purposeful leadership and deliberate design. We only see these cultures created and sustained when they are a true and honest reflection of the founders' attitudes, values, and activities.

It is essential to understand the effect of thoughtful culture design isn't confined to only those within the organization. According to Denise Lee Yohn's book *Fusion*, the best brands intentionally integrate their brand with their culture

(Yohn 2018). This suggests that internal cultures can and *will* dictate the organization's brand, which is why human capital experts often repeat the mantra, "Your employees are your first customers."

Founders who are genuinely committed to building diverse teams and designing cultures to support them will undoubtedly have a competitive edge, as they have the potential to create products, services, and experiences encompassing a much broader customer base.

We must remember, however, that brands are built from the inside out. Tiffani Bova summed this up well while serving as chief growth evangelist at Salesforce: "The fastest way to get customers to love your brand is to get employees to love their jobs" (Holloway and Armstrong 2020, 10).

Make no mistake, this is much easier said than done. But, with effort, it *can* be done.

# Chapter summary

- Eighty percent of company culture can be attributed to the founder/core leader.
- While culture is often not a priority in new organizations, it absolutely should be!
- Designing cultures for diverse teams is not easy, but the payoff is enormous.
- An organization's culture is a critical driver for its brand. As such, founders should think of their employees as their first customers.
- Founders committed to designing cultures for diverse teams will have a competitive advantage.

## CHAPTER 2

# CHECK YOUR BLIND SPOTS

My sons enjoy bird watching, so they frequently monitor the skies. Occasionally, we will see a large group of birds neatly lined up along the power lines, and one of my sons will point and say, "Look at all those birds!"

Invariably, I'll respond, "Maybe they're having a bird party."

The "bird party" is a reference to an African folktale. In the story, an unscrupulous tortoise convinces a group of birds to give him feathers so he can attend a bird party high in the sky. However, after tricking the birds who helped him, the tortoise finds himself featherless and falling through the air. His shell breaks into many pieces, which he eventually glues back together. According to the tale, this is the reason the tortoise's shell looks the way it does now.

At its core, this is a morality story about how we treat other people. But there is also an important lesson here about not striving to be someone other than who you are, a particularly essential lesson for founders.

As discussed in chapter one, 80 percent of an organization's culture is a reflection of the core leaders. Note that I am referring to a reflection of who you *are* as a leader, not who you *think* you should be. In other words, an organization built by the tortoise in our folktale will have a culture reflective of tortoise traits, not of the birds he tried to imitate.

Sometimes, seeing what is really there requires looking past what is apparent. According to US Bureau of Labor statistics, over 47 million people voluntarily left their jobs in 2021 alone, a trend aptly called the "Great Resignation" (Penn and Nezamis 2022). Within this trend lies another equally interesting one. Between January 2020 and October 2021, there was a 7 percent uptick in people leaving their jobs because of retirement (Tanzi 2022). As many as ten thousand boomers reach the retirement age of sixty-five each day (Fry 2019). So, even though baby boomers appear to be working longer than previous generations, it is certainly fair to say the US is on the cusp of yet another major workforce shift (Fry 2019).

In his 2014 TED Talk, Rainer Strack, senior partner emeritus and senior advisor for Boston Consulting Group, described this shift as the "workforce crisis of 2030." He, of course, could not have predicted the COVID-19 pandemic would accelerate the onset of the "Great Retirement," a phenomenon that, according to Strack, would trigger labor shortages in the largest economies across the globe. Notably, though, he highlighted this trend would not simply be a matter of fewer overall workers. Instead, it would be an exodus of the boomer generation's collective knowledge and skills that technology alone could not replace (Strack 2014).

I came across Strack's TED Talk in 2022 and was astounded by the accuracy of his predictions, even with the rising dependence on artificial intelligence to deliver more with fewer people. What was especially striking for me, though, was his caution that as the Great Retirement kicks into full force, business leaders will need to activate talent pools that have historically been underrepresented in the corporate workforce as well as lure some baby boomers out of retirement (Strack 2014). As someone writing a book on building organizational cultures for diverse teams, this recommendation made me smile.

In chapter one, I introduced the hypothetical (for now) reality show *Top Host* and the idea that to design organization cultures based on the diversity of guest list two, these founders must recognize that: 1) their organization's culture will be a reflection of who they are; and 2) designing a culture for a diverse team will require intentional effort.

When we consider the seismic impact the Great Retirement will have, founders who want to intentionally build organizational cultures for diverse teams become particularly valuable. In fact, founders who can successfully do so during this shift in the workforce stand to have a competitive advantage in the talent marketplace. If, according to Strack, these leaders can activate historically underrepresented groups in unique and differentiated ways, they can potentially achieve outsized success in the market (Strack 2014). I say "potentially" because a high-performing, highly engaged, diverse team will not offset a flawed business model or mistimed product launch. It can, however, help a founder to identify and address these challenges quickly.

If the Great Retirement and the ensuing need to activate underrepresented talent pools wasn't enough of a tailwind for these founders, then Generation Z—individuals born from 1997 through 2002—should provide an additional boost (Dimock 2019). While not quite as large as the baby boomer generation, they hold an important distinction: Gen Zers are the most racially and ethnically diverse generation of Americans *ever*. Almost half (48 percent) of Gen Zers identify as non-white, a significant increase from the boomers, only 18 percent of whom identify as non-white (Yuen 2021).

As a younger and more diverse generation enters the workforce, the "stock" of founders committed to building organizational cultures specifically geared toward diverse teams will only continue to gain value. If effective, these founders will stand out just like the *Top Host* finalist who can create a dining experience for the bombastically diverse guest list two. To achieve this, however, these leaders must be radically honest about themselves. Remember, an organization's culture will be primarily driven by who the core leaders are, not who they want to be. Part of this honesty comes from a recognition of one's blind spots.

When I refer to "blind spots," I am referring to an understanding of an individual's strengths and weaknesses regarding skills required to lead. I use this framing with founders because they, in particular, will need to use their blind spots as a lens through which to build out their teams. Put differently, one of the first steps to creating a culture for a diverse team is for the founder to surround themselves with individuals who have skills and experiences that they lack. By doing this, the founder is intentionally building a team in a manner that makes its diverse composition a prerequisite for success.

Throughout this book, I will refer to this type of executive as 15° Founders. I coined this term as a reference to a fun fact I stumbled upon during the latter waves of the pandemic.

Throughout 2020, as the COVID-19 pandemic dictated many aspects of our daily experience. I, like many, found I was doing a lot less driving overall. By the following year, I noticed I had to be much more conscientious about driving. My inner autopilot was utterly out of whack. I was making wrong turns on the way to visit friends whose homes I'd driven to countless times.

As such, I had to give a level of attentiveness to driving akin to when first learning. Around this time, I came across a piece of information that has forever changed how I drive. According to driving experts, turning the side mirrors out by about fifteen degrees, such that there is no visual overlap between the side mirrors and the rearview mirror, is the best way to virtually eliminate the blind spot (Parker and Igielnik 2020). I put this recommendation into practice right away and found it to be jarring at first: I had to get used to relying on each mirror for a unique view of the road around me. Once I adjusted, however, I liked having the expanded field of view.

When building a team, 15° Founders use a similar approach. They surround themselves with people whose skills and experiences give them an expanded field of view to rely upon for leading the organization. Paula Sneed, CEO of Phelps Prescott Group LLC and former executive vice president at Kraft Foods, is a phenomenal example. In the fall of 2022, I had the opportunity to meet with Sneed and hear her thoughts on what it means to build and lead diverse teams.

Anyone who knows Sneed knows her as unapologetically authentic and a truly incredible host. When asked how she approached hiring throughout her time as an executive, Sneed quickly mentioned that having teams with deep and broad strengths is important. And while she certainly understood her strengths and skills, she also understood the areas where she wasn't as strong.

A self-described "big ideas person who knows how to get things done," she admitted she did not enjoy dealing directly with myriad details. While recognizing the importance of having team members who had mastered their domains, she also specifically sought out individuals who were excellent in areas that were not in her zone of genius. Sometimes, she admitted, her natural tendencies and those of some of her team members were at odds, but this did not signify any real trouble. Sneed emphasized, "My comfort wasn't the goal. Having a great team that delivered results was!"

This is precisely how 15° Founders should approach hiring talent. Sneed's awareness of her strengths and weaknesses, what she liked and disliked, and even the types of personalities that got under her skin were the precise pieces of information she needed to make informed decisions about who should surround her. She intentionally covered her blind spots with the folks she selected.

Sneed's insights also highlight an important truth about building diverse teams: It will be uncomfortable. Too often, those in charge will optimize their teams for "fit," driven by the desire to make the leadership experience easier. But 15° Founders must be comfortable with discomfort—because building a culture around a diverse team will not be easy. It will, however, be worth the effort.

Demographic shifts will soon make it abundantly clear to leaders across the country that deploying diverse teams is no longer a well-meaning yet optional social impact initiative. Instead, it is mission-critical for successful business outcomes. Case in point: 80 percent of job seekers aged eighteen through thirty-four report a company's investment in diversity, equity, and inclusion is essential to them when considering a new job (Terrazas and Johnson 2022). In essence, they are seeking organizations built by 15° Founders.

## Chapter summary

- The Great Retirement, accelerated by the COVID-19 pandemic, will bring significant shifts to the US workforce and will require leaders to activate historically underrepresented talent pools.
- Leaders who intentionally build organizational cultures optimized for diverse teams will be better positioned to compete for the best talent.
- Successfully building an organizational culture for a diverse team requires a leader to be very clear on who they are and are not, so they can cover their blind spots.
- The 15° Founders are leaders who are aware of their blind spots and build teams that balance out those weaknesses.
- Being a 15° Founder will be an uncomfortable but worthwhile journey.

## CHAPTER 3

# DESIGN YOUR CULTURE FROM THE INSIDE OUT

---

## Commemorating Dagen H

On September 3, 1967, at precisely 5:00 a.m., drivers in Sweden tuned in to a radio countdown, signaling the country's official shift from driving on the left-hand side of the road to driving on the right-hand side (Martin 2017). As drivers listened to "Håll dig till höger, Svensson"—translated as "Keep on the Right, Svensson" and written as part of the PR campaign to remind drivers of the significant shift—Sweden's Högertrafikomläggningen (translated as "right-hand traffic diversion") or Dagen H ("H Day") was born (Savage 2018).

As it turns out, Sweden was not alone in this endeavor. Between 1919 and 1984, thirty-four countries transitioned from "left-hand traffic" to driving on the right hand side (World Population Review 2022). For these thirty-four countries, the process of making this transition was herculean. Everything from road signage, the design of cars and buses, traffic signals, road markings, road etiquette, and even the way people learned to drive had to change.

In short, for each of those countries to achieve its desired outcome, the entire driving culture had to change in very intentional ways.

For this to happen in Sweden, the leadership had to first be clear on its goals. By 1967, Sweden's neighbors were already right-hand traffic countries. Hence, Sweden's government decided that switching sides was a critical way to reduce traffic accidents and facilitate more accessible cross-border travel, thereby keeping its citizens safe (Savage 2018).

It's important to note here the push to shift public behavior came *after* the commitment to public safety as the overall effort's core value. For 15° Founders, understanding that values must be clear before behaviors can be changed is equally essential.

Let's return briefly to our televised competition scenario. Like the countries that decided to shift from left-hand traffic to right-hand traffic, contestants in *Top Host* must be clear about the desired results: impress judges like you by crafting a world-class dining experience.

Before they can impress the judges, though, the hosts must first impress the guests attending each dinner. Similarly, before 15° Founders can create a brand that resonates with their intended external customers, they must first create a culture that resonates with their internal team members.

## CULTŪRA

I created the CULTŪRA framework to walk 15° Founders through the five-step process of crafting a thoughtful culture for an organization in its early stages. The framework can also be used for mature organizations looking for a cultural overhaul. However, it must be noted that for these organizations, significant attention must also be given to the gap between existing culture and desired culture and the steps required to move across that chasm.

## CULTŪRA *Framework* for Culture Design

**CU**stomer Value

Clearly define the value your organization will create for customers

**L**ink Core Values

Link your organization's core values to the value you will create for customers

**T**ie Values to Behaviors

Define the specific behaviors that reflect the organization's core values

**U**nderscore with **R**ecognition

Recognize and reward behaviors that reflect the organization's core values

**A**ctivate with Belonging

Activate leadership, facilitator(s), shared elements and experiences, and rituals to foster belonging

The framework is designed to help 15° Founders first clarify what the organization has to offer to its customers before designing a culture that will enable its diverse team members to bring that vision to life. In the next section, I will describe each step of the framework and provide examples of how to action these steps.

## Start with your customer

According to Vineet Nayar, author of *Employees First, Customers Second*, the only way to create an exceptional and differentiated customer experience is to first create a unique and differentiated employee experience (Moore 2012). Furthermore, according to a 2021 *Harvard Business Review* article, companies that prioritize their employees to create an optimal customer experience achieve 1.8 times faster revenue growth than those that do not (Solis 2021).

The COVID-19 pandemic brought this to light in many ways. Many of us experienced as customers the direct effects of both thoughtful and thoughtless employee experiences for the businesses in our respective communities.

Research suggests the leader is especially critical to the employee experience for small businesses—more so than in larger, more established companies. According to a 2020 *Forbes Insights* report, "The Experience Equation: How Happy Employees and Customers Accelerate Growth," conducted in partnership with Salesforce, strong leadership and the right culture can lead to high-growth scenarios for small businesses that deepen employee engagement (Holloway and Armstrong 2020, 14).

This suggests that 15° Founders are uniquely positioned to establish cultural landscapes that will supercharge the employee experience and, thus, the organization's ability to create value for customers. Make no mistake, the founder must still be able to identify a timely and relevant market opportunity and attract the right capital to execute that opportunity.

But, as is the case with *Top Host*, our contestants' guests must be the first champions and evangelists, and this can only happen if the 15° Founder can build a great culture around them.

The question, of course, is how exactly 15° Founders should do this, particularly when constructing diverse teams. In his 2009 TEDx talk, which has since been viewed over sixty million times, Simon Sinek provides some key insights. Based on his book *Start with Why*, Sinek repeatedly indicates that "people don't buy what you do, they buy why you do it" (Sinek 2009).

The first component of the CULTURA framework is the customer—because 15° Founders must be clear about *why* the issue they are trying to solve even matters to them. Clarifying this helps founders define their organization's mission and vision.

By mission, I'm referring to precisely why the company exists and what specific problem it addresses. By vision, I am referring to the unique future-state role the organization will play in customers' lives as it works toward the mission. In the lexicon of Peter Diamandis, serial entrepreneur and founder of the XPRIZE Foundation, 15° Founders can think of this as the massive transformational purpose for their organization (Diamandis, n.d.).

Defining this "why" is a critical step: It will underpin the culture they design. It is the soil on which the culture will be built.

I use the term "soil" here because *cultura* is a Latin word meaning to till or cultivate, as when caring for plants (Mahoney 2023). The CULTŪRA framework was named with this in mind—that designing a culture requires constant cultivation. Organizational cultures are very much alive and must be rooted in something. For 15° Founders, the commitment to serving customers' needs with a truly diverse team must be mindfully embedded in the cultural soil and continually nurtured by the leaders.

## Link core values to customer value

Once the 15° Founder can articulate the organization's reason for existing and who they want to be for customers in a future state, they can then reflect on the values underpinning their mission and vision. Values define how things are done and serve as critical guideposts for how the 15° Founder wants to address potential needs. Moreover, once the founder has answered how the organization will show up for customers, they can link this outcome to how it will show up for employees.

We've often heard the term customer-obsessed tossed around as the key to boundless success in business. While I don't disagree with this orientation, it's essential to understand who your first customer is: your employees.

You must first convince employees of the value you can create with your product or service. In *Top Host*, the dinner guests will be the first champions and evangelists for each host-contestant. Similarly, employee viewpoints will ultimately translate into the product or service you offer to your customers.

Remember that for 15° Founders, core values serve as a significant opportunity to embed a commitment to diversity and inclusion into the cultural soil. This comes from recognizing the team's diverse composition is a crucial ingredient to the success of the overall venture. Ellen Bailey, vice president of diversity and culture at Harvard Business Publishing, offers keen insights on what it takes to make this happen.

> Do what's right, even when it's hard.
>
> —ELLEN BAILEY

I met Bailey in November 2022 and had the opportunity to discuss the creation of Harvard Business Publishing's diversity and culture function with her. This function was born in the aftermath of the murder of George Floyd and what we now consider the early waves of the COVID-19 pandemic.

It was a challenging period in Bailey's career and for the organization. Circumstances notwithstanding, Bailey followed her mantra: "Do what's right, even when it's hard." Once Bailey began building the function, however, she quickly realized the organization needed to refashion its core values to truly honor their belief in diversity and inclusion, both internally and externally.

Revisiting and ultimately revising Harvard Business Publishing's core values allowed her to begin embedding a commitment to diversity, equity, and inclusion within the organizational culture. "Our culture impacts everything," Bailey reflected.

The same is true for any organization. Culture reaches far and wide, and as such, thoughtfulness around that culture's core values is paramount. Harvard Business Publishing is a global brand with a mission to improve the practice of management in a changing world (*Harvard Business Review*, n.d.).

Achieving this mission requires the organization to consider diverse opinions, and Bailey is helping ensure they accomplish that mission inside and out.

## Tie values to behaviors

Once 15° Founders have defined their core values based on what they want customers to affiliate with the organization (i.e., brand values), they must clearly articulate behaviors that reflect these tenets.

For many leaders, this step may seem like a non-critical activity. However, I have consistently found this to be a transformative exercise for 15° Founders. The reason is that aligning on the organization's mission, vision, and values is necessary but insufficient for creating an intentional, high-performing, inclusive culture.

Founders must clearly define the desired behaviors to demonstrate the company's values within the context of their specific culture. These behaviors will propel the culture forward and should materially distinguish your organization, so it's essential to be thoughtful in defining what they are and why they matter.

In addition to defining these behaviors, you, the 15° Founder, must also institute them by actually modeling what they look like. As the leader, everything you say and do will resonate across the organization, and this resonance is most potent when the "say-do ratio" (i.e., the ratio of things you say you'll do to the things you do) is high.

# A good report from school

I had a firsthand encounter with behaviors that reflect cultural values on a typical day while picking up my son from school. I was greeted by the after-school teacher, who pulled me aside and told me she wanted to brag about my son's behavior.

*What?* I thought. *I'm so here for this.*

She began by explaining how, when it was time for the kids to transition to the next activity, the boys in the class refused to help clean up. Several claimed they didn't need to clean up because the girls were supposed to do that. My son, thankfully, told the other boys that cleaning wasn't "just for the girls to do" and was the only boy who helped with the mess.

It was a proud mom moment.

But something about it bothered me as I gave my son a fist bump and we went to the car. When we got home, I told the story to my husband, and he gave me a look. "Exactly," I said. "Where did seven- and eight-year-old boys from different homes get the idea that, in this school setting, they were exempt from cleaning *and*, specifically, that the girls should clean up after them?" With this question on repeat in my head, I started paying more attention at school, particularly during morning drop-off.

What I saw the very next morning slapped me in the face. Like many schools, a fairly elaborate procedure had been designed to create an orderly process for getting kids out of cars and into the building. For the first time, I noticed there did appear to be gendered roles in how the morning procedures worked: The male teachers and administrators stood around and monitored traffic flow while the female staff got the kids out of cars and on their way.

When I entered the administration office, the folks behind the desk were female while the leaders were overwhelmingly male. Even in assemblies and other events, gender roles were evident. It became clear to me the kids in my son's class were observing and mimicking the behaviors seen in the school environment. Unfortunately, those behaviors likely were not communicating the school's core values the way the administrators and, certainly, my son's teacher wanted them to.

## Underscore with recognition

If you've ever been to a birthday party for preschoolers or spent time in a preschool classroom, you've likely seen this scenario play out. One child builds something with magnetic blocks, and all the adults swoon over the creation. Instantly, half the kids in the room swarm the magnetic blocks, and every single one of them will create something over which a grown-up better swoon… or else. I'd argue adults often do the same thing—we're just marginally better at being less blatant.

The 15° Founders must tap into the inner preschooler within us all by understanding that what gets recognized and rewarded gets replicated. So, in addition to defining and modeling behaviors that embody the organization's core values, leaders must be thoughtful about recognizing and rewarding these behaviors in others so they can be replicated across the organization.

Let's look at an example of a small business that is actively working to get this right.

# The Next Street way

Next Street Financial is a mission-driven advisory firm providing a suite of advisory, tech, and strategic solutions designed to support entrepreneurs and small businesses, particularly those who have historically faced disproportionate barriers. When chatting with Charisse Conanan Johnson, one of the company's co-CEOs, it became clear they are an excellent example of linking brand values to core values then defining and rewarding behaviors that embody them.

Johnson is an author, a fintech entrepreneur, and a former investment banker who is passionate about Next Street's mission and principles. According to Johnson, Next Street was founded in 2006 as a B-Corp committed to supporting small businesses through advisory services.

Notably, their core values focused on integrity, commitment to excellence, and making sure everyone's voice was heard. Small businesses weren't explicitly called out, though it was internally understood they were at the core of this mission-oriented company.

So when Johnson and her two co-CEOs, Samantha Berg and Michael Roth, took over in 2020, they decided to revisit this core to create an even stronger alignment with how they show up for the small businesses they serve.

Next Street is overt in externally communicating its core values of anti-racist, authentic joy, bias toward action, interwoven and empowered sustainable growth, and small businesses first (Next Street 2022). When asked about the anti-racist value, Johnson indicated, "It was hard to do our work without calling it [racism] out very clearly."

As such, Next Street has worked both internally and externally to exemplify anti-racist action, and this commitment shows up in everything from how proposals are written to hiring decisions. There is even an internal team, the Inclusive Impact Committee, designed to keep the organization accountable to this core value.

When I asked Johnson how she and the executive team at Next Street recognize and reward behaviors that align with their core values, she indicated they allocated part of the annual budget to do so. In my work with Next Street, I had the opportunity to see this up close.

In particular, the company gives spot bonuses to team members who do outstanding work in a manner that reflects the company's values. Nominations must include the value being reflected and a description of how the team member's work meets that value. Since the bonus amounts are sizable, this program serves as an effective mechanism for incentivizing value-aligned behaviors.

As we see in the CULTŪRA framework, it isn't enough to define great, differentiated core values. Leaders must ensure those values are linked to behaviors that can be modeled, rewarded, and, ultimately, reinforced. Next Street not only defined its beliefs, but according to Johnson, they invest financially to reward corresponding behaviors.

This has resulted in a truly diverse organization that takes their mission and values very seriously. Between 2020 and 2022, Next Street experienced tremendous business growth and a 90 percent retention rate despite the Great Resignation. Their formula is clearly working!

**What gets recognized and rewarded
gets replicated.**

## Activate with belonging

The final component of the CULTŪRA framework is to activate with belonging. The 15° Founders who have earned their employees' trust can and should create high-belonging cultures. They must recognize, though, that designing belonging for diverse teams requires more intention and thoughtfulness than for more homogenous teams.

According to *Merriam-Webster*, "belonging" can be defined as a close or intimate relationship (*Merriam-Webster* 2023). I like this definition for two reasons: First, it's simple; and second, it reminds me of the early days of Meta in which updating one's status to "In a Relationship" was considered a grand gesture.

Belonging at work happens when leaders have established a baseline of trust with their team members and created an environment in which they experience actual psychological safety.

Psychological safety, the belief that one can speak up without punishment or humiliation, was added to the modern lexicon by Amy Edmondson, the Novartis Professor of Leadership and Management at Harvard University (Edmonson and Mortensen 2021). According to an interview with Edmonson, someone with a sense of belonging within their organization believes, "This is a place where I can thrive. I feel that I am truly a member of the community" (HBS Working Knowledge 2018).

The importance of belonging can't be overstated—this isn't just about ensuring team members feel the organization is friendly to them. It is about ensuring these team members are able to bring forward the diverse perspectives you hired them for. To illustrate, it helps to consider what happens when team members do *not* experience belonging. Melissa Franklin, diversity and inclusion expert and dear friend, put it this way:

> *If you have people in your organization who do not feel they belong because they aren't experiencing the psychological safety to share their true feelings about what they may be experiencing at work or even personally, you should assume those folks are also not sharing their true feelings about the projects they are on. As such, the organization is not getting the best quality out of those team members, which will negatively impact the quality of the organization's products and services.*

Next Street Financial provides a clever example of this. Anyone visiting their website will see the company's commitment to serving small business owners, particularly those who have historically faced disproportionate barriers. Here's the thing, though—Next Street's website is the first company website I've ever seen that features small businesses owned by *employees.*

Essentially, Next Street is declaring its identity as a company that both serves small business owners and is comprised of many small business owners. The company has attached itself to the identity of "small business owner" at a corporate level in a way that, importantly, is designed to foster belonging between its customers and employees.

The ability to foster belonging for truly diverse teams is central to what distinguishes 15° Founders from other leaders. It is also the secret weapon that enables high-performing, innovative teams. As such, fostering belonging is mission-critical for 15° Founders because they cannot afford *not* to have high-quality input from the varied array of perspectives on their team. In the next chapter, we'll discuss the key ingredients these leaders must have to successfully activate belonging.

The CULTŪRA framework serves both as a playbook and a diagnostic tool for 15°Founders seeking to build high-performing, high-belonging cultures for their diverse teams. As a playbook, the framework will guide them through the design of their organizational cultures. As a diagnostic tool, it enables 15° Founders to identify where there may be challenges with the culture and pinpoint things to address.

In both cases, founders must remember their organizations' cultures are continuously nurtured by what they pour into them.

## Chapter summary

- When designing an organization's culture, 15° Founders must remember their employees are their first customers.
- Your organization's culture is the link between the employee and customer experiences.
- A high-performing, high-belonging culture built around a diverse team never happens by accident. It results from a leader who has intentionally designed it and embedded diversity as one of its core values.
- The CULTŪRA framework can help 15° Founders navigate the intentional culture design process.

## CHAPTER 4

# THE SECRET SAUCE OF BELONGING

———

I must confess that I *love* weddings and everything about them. I enjoy the energy that surrounds the ritual, the fact it's one of few occasions when we can see entire communities take the time to come together, and that the experience is typically a powerful reflection of the cultures of the two people tying the knot. Not to mention, how often do you get the opportunity to see friends and family dress to impress? I'm so here for it.

I've attended a decent number of weddings, but looking back, one in particular stands out aside from my own: One of my closest friends from college gave me the full Eritrean wedding experience. From the orthodox church service and the ululation to the traditional Eritrean food and multi-generational dance party, she welcomed her college friends to this wedding ritual not as guests but as community members. In other words, my friend's wedding was a shared experience that enabled attendees to experience belonging among the community of individuals invited to celebrate.

Belonging is a hot topic in organizations of all sizes because leaders are beginning to understand (with the support of a growing body of research) that this can be a vital determinant of the employee experience. It is also a key component for retaining the best talent.

I became particularly interested in belonging during a period of reflection on my career and personal journey. At the time, I'd been in a company where my direct leaders changed every year, which was considered typical across the organization. I noticed that with each leadership change, a "reset" button was pressed on how much I experienced belonging. I was curious as to why, and I often wondered whether or not I could intentionally (and quickly) engineer belonging on any team I led. After exploring the topic for a few years, I arrived at three fundamental principles.

### Principle 1:
### Yes, you can design belonging, but only if you mean it... for real.

First, belonging can only be cultivated once the founder has built trust with the team. There's truly no way around this. According to Dr. Brené Brown's book *Dare to Lead*, trust is built in micro-moments that can happen at any time (Brown 2018). In other words, trust is being built—or broken—in the seemingly mundane day-to-day interactions with your team, not when making grand presentations. Trust is closely linked to integrity, something we'll discuss more in chapter eight.

Like building trust, cultivating belonging is a continual process that is "always on" (Gonzales 2022). So, as I do with most things, I began seeking examples of high-belonging communities around me, hoping to identify insights outside the corporate setting. As I did this, four ingredients showed up again and again.

1. Leaders
2. Facilitators
3. Shared experiences and elements
4. Rituals

Let's consider how each of these four ingredients supports Principle 1.


## Leaders

The first ingredient to a high-belonging environment is the leader. Without exception, this leader is critical to ensuring that belonging is a community priority—because they effectively decreed that it would be so. Additionally, the senior leader sets the expectation that all the organization's other leaders are held accountable for prioritizing this. This was particularly true with 15° Founders committed to ensuring their organizations cultivated belonging among all members, not just the loudest or most prominent. These leaders made their vision a reality by conferring authority to facilitators.


## Facilitators

Facilitators are those we often call the "glue" in a high-belonging organization. In small organizations, they may also be leaders, but the roles are very distinct. With the leader's support, facilitators are the ones who repeatedly extend the "invitation" for team members to belong. They are the organization's "culture captains" and often make themselves first to meet new hires. If a leader is intentional, this role is acknowledged and formalized in some way. Too often, though, facilitators can be informal or self-appointed (e.g., "Naghmeh has been here the longest, so she's the one who shows everyone the ropes").

Great facilitators do three things.

1. They champion and often engineer accessible, inclusive shared experiences.
2. They lead rituals that reinforce belonging within the community.
3. They use their role as facilitators to support the overall organization, not themselves.

True facilitators do not position themselves as gatekeepers wielding the power of social capital at their discretion. Instead, they promote shared elements that create opportunities for those in the community to uniquely identify and communicate with each other without the assistance of the facilitator. They are connectors, not blockers.

> They are connectors, not blockers.

### Shared experiences and elements

Shared experiences and elements are where we will see most facilitators at work, and we will see a wide range in any given organization. Still, the most effective ones are those that are both accessible and inclusive. This means that within the context of a diverse business, these experiences and elements require no prerequisites, and all community members are explicitly invited to participate. Examples here are team events that require no shared interests, such as improvisation classes, escape rooms, picnics, etc., or even shared symbols (e.g., company "lingo") that are unique to the community and meant to be understood by all its members.

Shared history is a specific type of element that is particularly effective in designing a high-belonging culture. While we often think of this in a familial sense, there are myriad examples of its power in professional settings.

Paula Sneed, CEO of Phelps Prescott Group LLC and former executive vice president at Kraft Foods, shares an example of this when recounting her experiences in managing Kraft's dessert division: "I knew the history of the brands in my division—who started them, how they were made, all of it."

So when Sneed managed the division, she recognized she'd become part of the legacy of those brands, and this historical connection to the brands amplified her impact beyond her time in the role.

Similarly, when joining the military or even in school settings, initiation rituals may require new members to learn the organization's history, wear specific colors, or even say certain phrases to internalize the idea they've become a part of something bigger than themselves. As with all shared experiences and elements, the only prerequisite is membership and the desire to belong.

## Rituals

Rituals are specific types of shared experiences that typically mark milestones—induction into the community, key accomplishments, life events, etc. For high-belonging organizations, rituals are led by facilitators and used similarly. They mark key milestones reinforcing one's community membership. Examples could be a new hire ritual requiring new team members to introduce themselves while holding a beach ball or ringing a large gong when a salesperson closes a deal.

While they can often be easy to overlook, facilitators can use these events as micro-moments that nurture belonging between new and existing community members. Shared experiences and elements can be thought of as "always on." However, rituals are specific and distinct events. For this reason, they are typically few in number.

> Shared experiences and elements can be thought of as "always on." Rituals, however, are specific and distinct events.

In light of these four ingredients, one critical nuance of belonging mustn't be overlooked: similar to attending my friend's wedding, an invitation to belong must both be given and accepted. This means that while facilitators continually extend this invitation, team members must be willing to say yes.

Like cultivating trust, though, there may be a wide variance in how long it takes for someone to experience enough micro-moments to be convinced the invitation is genuine. Master facilitators, aware of this nuance, can use rituals and other shared experiences and elements to reinforce the invitation's authenticity for all individuals in a diverse organization.

*Principle 2:*
*Belonging is cultivated at the micro level,*
*not the macro level.*

The second principle to understand about belonging is *where* it is best fostered within an organization, a critical feature that can often be overlooked. In a company's early stages, the onus for building belonging will fall on the 15° Founder.

As the organization grows, this founder must distribute the responsibility among the leadership team (thereby making them facilitators) to ensure a cascading effect across the organization. This is because belonging is best fostered at the micro level—that is, at the level best aligned with where individuals have the most day-to-day interactions.

As the organization grows, 15° Founders must find ways to constantly ensure that while prioritizing belonging, the work needed to foster it continues to happen at the most granular team level. So, as the organization gets larger and more layered, belonging must continue to be fostered within each additional layer. Often, this is easier said than done. For this reason, I like to look outside business settings for examples of how 15° Founders can achieve this within their organizations.

## Sisterhood

One salient example of this for me came in the form of my older sister, who is easily one of the best belonging facilitators I know.

In the spring of 1997, my sister joined Delta Sigma Theta Sorority Incorporated, an organization founded in 1913 at

Howard University. Today, the organization boasts over 350,000 members across over a thousand chapters worldwide (Delta Sigma Theta Sorority, Inc. 2022), including notables such as Natalie Cole, Dr. Betty Shabazz, and Barbara Jordan (Ali 2016).

Delta Sigma Theta is among nine historically black sororities and fraternities governed by the National Pan-Hellenic Council. This organization was founded in 1930 when the existing governing body would not accept organizations with African-American members (National Pan-Hellenic Council 2022). Each of the nine sororities and fraternities in the council has distinctive logos and branding that allow members to find and identify each other quickly.

In observing my sister's time at college, I found a fantastic example of what it means to use shared experiences and elements at the micro level to engineer a sense of belonging within a global organization. The Delta Sigma Theta executive committee serves as the organization's international leader and has a vested interest in ensuring that all sorority sisters experience high belonging. Since members join through any of the over one thousand chapters worldwide, each chapter functions effectively as a micro-organization.

Like many sororities, new members join a chapter in discrete cohorts, with existing members responsible for bringing in new ones. These members, serving as facilitators, design shared experiences for each new cohort. Each cohort then participates in initiation rituals to solidify their membership in the organization.

As members navigate their lives and careers, there are always myriad invitations to join in the shared experiences of volunteering in community events or welcoming new members. Members can quickly identify each other through shared elements, including a specific crest commonly worn on clothing, hand gestures, a distinct call and response, and many others.

My sister still often serves as a belonging facilitator for her chapter. She plans their annual holiday party, inviting chapter members to participate in a yearly experience that will reinforce their sense of belonging and deepen their relationships with each other. Over twenty-five years after joining, my sister remains very close to her sorority sisters and still experiences a high sense of belonging within Delta Sigma Theta.

This organization is an excellent example of one that has sanctioned belonging as a priority at the leadership level but has also instituted mechanisms to ensure it is cultivated at the micro level, which, in this case, are chapters and new member cohorts within each chapter. I would go so far as to say this organization has engineered this so well for its over 350,000 members internationally that women who would otherwise be perfect strangers have been invited into a shared history, shared experiences, and shared elements that can enable them to quickly connect and engage as a true community of sisters for the rest of their lives.

For 15° Founders, this sorority serves as a great example of the power of incorporating belonging into an organization's foundation and the lasting impact this can have on its members. This organization is also an excellent example of the fact that when fostering belonging, size matters. According to British anthropologist Robin Dunbar, humans over time have formed communities of varying degrees of closeness at highly predictable group sizes—fifteen, fifty, one hundred fifty, five hundred, fifteen hundred, and so on (Han 2021). This is important because as an organization grows, a

15° Founder must recognize when it is time to create smaller divisions so that belonging can be more easily cultivated.

Delta Sigma Theta has been showing us how to do this for more than a hundred years.


***Principle 3:***
***A high degree of belonging within an organization can translate into a high-belonging experience for consumers.***


In chapter three, we discussed that employees are an organization's first customers. We also discussed culture as the link between the employee experience and the customer experience. As such, 15° Founders must recognize that a diverse group of employees who experience a high degree of belonging leads to a diverse, high-belonging group of customers.

As such, if an organization wants to strengthen the connection between its customers and its brand, it should start with the sense of belonging between its employees and the organization itself. In other words, they must think inside out.

To illustrate this principle, I'll use two examples.


**The Fortieth Reunion**

In May 2022, my mentor, Anaezi Modu, founder and CEO of REBRAND, was preparing to attend her fortieth class reunion at her alma mater, Princeton University. This year was particularly special because she was on the planning committee. The theme? "Epic belonging." Clearly, I needed to know more.

As I would later learn, Princeton's annual reunion weekend is a *thing*. A *really big thing*. When I asked Modu to describe the event, she chuckled and said, "Oh, it's madness!"

Princeton's ratio of undergraduate to graduate students is about 1.8:1, so many would describe the institution as very undergrad-focused (Princeton University 2023). As such, things go to new levels when it comes to alum engagement, particularly for those who did undergraduate degrees.

Universities like Princeton often plan alumni reunion events such that each graduating class would be invited back every five years (i.e., in 2025, they'd invite those who graduated in years ending in zero or five. In 2026, they'd invite those from years ending in one or six, and so on). While Princeton does use this approach, *all* alums are invited to return to campus to join the annual reunion events the weekend before commencement, even if it's not their official reunion year.

The highlight of the weekend is the P-rade, which first began in 1896 (Princeton University 2022). Members of each reunion class complete a mile-long procession led by the president, university officials, and members of the oldest graduating class. Classes join the P-rade in descending order so that each is cheered on by those who finished after them. The final group to join the procession is the current year's graduating class, which is then welcomed into the Princeton alum community by those who graduated before them. It's an incredible ritual that makes it easy to understand why the P-rade is such a big deal.

When I examined the P-rade, I couldn't help but dive deep into the photos. The eldest alumnus is given an honorary cane to celebrate their commitment to the university, and each class has a jacket that enables them to quickly identify each other (Princeton University 2022). As belonging facilitators, planning committee volunteers take on the arduous task of creating opportunities for their classmates to reconnect through shared event experiences.

The P-rade has become a display of epic belonging at its finest, but make no mistake, this isn't simply an annual accident. The university is committed to ensuring that once students graduate from Princeton, they remain deeply connected to the university as alumni who, ideally, will continue to support the institution in myriad ways.

Since Princeton students effectively transition from being "products" of the university to "customers" (e.g., individuals to contribute financially or otherwise in exchange for something of perceived value; here, an opportunity to invest in their alma mater's continued success and prestige), the university is incentivized to ensure the sense of belonging extends far beyond its classrooms. With this in mind, Princeton has designed an incredibly differentiated way to reactivate that sense of belonging among its alumni each year in a manner you may have to see to believe.

"Oooh, to be a Gooner..."

I met my husband while living and working in London in the early 2000s. Just a few months into dating, he gave me the first of many gifts—an Arsenal jersey with my name monogrammed on the back (which I still have). As a huge sports fan growing up, I loved the jersey. The only issue, of course, was that I had no idea who or what Arsenal was.

About a year later, we attended a preseason game against Paris Saint-Germain at the Emirates Stadium. By this time, I'd been fully baptized into English Premiership soccer. Still, nothing could have prepared me for the in-person experience. It was almost like being in a worship service at church, only world-class athletes had taken over the pulpit. There were specific Arsenal club songs and chants sung passionately throughout the experience, all in unison, by literally thousands of fans across the stadium. Never in my life had I seen anything like this.

While we often focus on players' experience on a team such as the Arsenal Football Club, the English Football League has a vested interest in ensuring fans—not just players—experience a high degree of belonging with each club. In my experience at Emirates Stadium, I, the gobsmacked, not-quite-soccer-fan, was invited to participate in the rituals endemic to Arsenal fandom.

What is so striking to me about the English Premiership Football League is that they have crafted the fan experience to cultivate loyalty and a sense of belonging with the *clubs*, not individual players. As such, fans like my husband identify themselves by the club they support, not the players they root for. That sense of belonging is cultivated by the shared experience of watching games with other fans, whether in a stadium, a sports bar, or even in friends' homes across the globe.

Belonging for English Premiership Football fans can be reinforced with monogrammed club jerseys featuring the wearer's name on the back so that any and every Arsenal fan can proudly identify themselves and each other. Since receiving my first monogrammed jersey, I've met people whose Premiership club loyalties were multi-generational. I've even met folks who, according to my husband, were great people but, unfortunately, were "Manchester United supporters."

(As of the writing of this book, my sons had received their first monogrammed Arsenal jerseys, so I fully expect our own multi-generational allegiance to continue.)

Crafting belonging for a diverse team is as much art as science. It will require persistence and a genuine commitment to continue extending the invitation to belong. As a 15° Founder, it is essential you and your core leaders understand its importance and that you are unwavering in using each of the four ingredients to foster it.

As you navigate this process for your organization, some trial and error will likely be involved. Just remember that when using the four ingredients, your resulting flavor of belonging should be unique to your organization. As we see with Delta Sigma Theta, Princeton University, and the English Premiership Football League, if 15° Founders keep the three principles of belonging in mind, they have the power to cultivate a high degree of belonging inside and outside the organization itself.

> Crafting belonging for a diverse team
> is as much art as science.

**Belonging in action: A thought exercise**

Ade Omitowoju is an entrepreneur, investor, and serves as a managing director at the Black Venture Capital Consortium (BVCC), a firm committed to closing the racial wealth gap by increasing the number of black professionals in venture capital and tech.

Not only does this venture fund manage a portfolio to generate returns for its investors, BVCC also partners with historically black colleges and universities (HBCUs) to identify top-performing students interested in careers in finance and tech, and places them at any of their thirty-plus venture capital firms and twelve tech companies.

According to the non-profit BLCK VC, only 3 percent of venture capital investors and 2 percent of partners at venture firms are black (BLCK VC 2022). Similarly, according to the US Equal Opportunity Commission, black professionals account for 7.4 percent of the tech workforce (US Equal Employment Opportunity Commission, n.d.) despite being 13.6 percent of the U.S. population, according to the US Census Bureau (US Census Bureau, n.d.).

So, more often than not, the students who participate in BVCC's internships and fellowships will be among very few black team members at their host companies.

Now, let's imagine you can step into a prominent leadership position at one of these host companies, and one of the BVCC interns is assigned to your team. How might you engage them in a manner that fosters belonging?

In this case, you'd want to start designing a high-belonging experience even before the intern joins the team. One should never underestimate the power of a well-crafted note or a thoughtful phone call inviting them to belong by highlighting the value they will bring to the team.

Once the intern joins up, you can intentionally communicate the vision and values for your team, which should directly relate to those of the organization. You'll also want to explicitly share the behaviors you are cultivating and (hopefully) modeling for your team. All of this can be part of a thoughtful onboarding ritual.

Remember, it is critically important to follow through in cultivating values and behaviors. For example, suppose a desired behavior is for team members to share their insight on potential investments. In that case, this may mean asking for the intern's opinion, waiting for it to be shared, and then recognizing them for sharing regardless of the idea itself. The intent here is to recognize the behaviors you want to propagate and simultaneously begin to engender trust through micro-moments.

Lastly, use shared elements as a reminder of the intern's belonging to the group. Company swag is often an obvious go-to for this, but consider what other shared elements could symbolize belonging within your team. These could include walking the intern through the team's or company's history and highlighting their role in this journey or inviting them to participate in group rituals throughout their internship. Keep in mind the only criteria for engaging in these shared experiences should be team membership, not shared interests.

# Chapter summary

- Belonging can be thought of as an invitation that must be both offered and accepted.
- Belonging can be engineered based on these three principles:
    - Yes, you can design belonging, but only if you mean it… for real.
    - Belonging is cultivated at the micro level, not the macro level.
    - A high degree of belonging within an organization, done well, can translate into a high-belonging experience for your customers.
- Within the first principle, there are four ingredients needed to cultivate organizational belonging:
    - Leaders
    - Facilitators
    - Shared experiences and elements
    - Rituals

# BREATHE LIFE INTO YOUR CULTURE THROUGH COMMUNICATION— PART 1

Have you ever been startled by how different families communicate with each other?

I was born and raised in Dallas, Texas. My father is Ghanaian, and my mother is African-American. When it came to communication norms, my mom essentially set the standard. If we needed to convey an opinion, we prided ourselves on the strength of the logic forming the basis of that opinion. No one ever stated out loud that emotions had no place in our discussions. Instead, it was just understood that emotions should be kept in check and only used when appropriate. There was generally never a reason to yell unless there was a fire or a worship service in church.

So there I was, minding my business and going about my merry life. And then, one day, I went to Lagos, Nigeria, to meet my now-husband's family for the first time.

On the afternoon of our arrival, several family members were gathered around the dining table. From my vantage point, everyone was yelling at each other. *Everyone.* Initially, I thought something was very wrong since, based on my family context, that was just about the only logical reason I could fathom for why everyone was yelling. As I stood there, nervously blinking, it finally dawned on me that—in fact—everyone was ecstatic to be together. They simply had a communication style that was different from my family's.

Our respective families illustrate two very different ways of engaging, both anchored in a genuine desire to show love and support. It's noteworthy, though, that the different communication models are primarily a function of the culture defined by our parents in our respective homes.

As a 15°Founder, you can breathe life into your culture through your communication, which will extend to employees and, ultimately, your customers. Remember, your employees are your first customers. As such, communication that enlivens your culture internally will directly translate into how your brand comes to life externally.

Your culture comes to life<br>through your communication.

Considering the CULTŪRA framework introduced in chapter three, each facet of defining the organization's culture requires thoughtful communication. Determining the brand experience you want customers to have and the values that underpin that identity will ultimately dictate how you communicate to your customers. As you link brand values to internal core tenets, tie those values to desired behaviors, underscore those behaviors with recognition, and activate the culture through belonging. Executing each of these steps requires thoughtful communication.

In business and life, getting communication right is paramount to successful outcomes. Too often, though, there is a mismatch between the desired culture and the actual culture perpetuated by the leaders' communication. This mismatch can be very costly.

According to the *MIT Sloan Management Review*, a 2020 study conducted on 562 large, primarily US organizations with published statements on corporate culture found that integrity, collaboration, and culture were the most recurring values mentioned. However, when this information was compared to a sentiment analysis of the nine most commonly cited core values based on Glassdoor reviews by employees of those same companies, there was no correlation between the publicly stated values and the employees' perceptions of the company's values (Sull, Turconi, and Sull 2020).

This research was done on large organizations, so it's fair to suspect that smaller, early-stage companies may have an advantage here. That said, the study suggests it is much easier than leaders may think to find their perceptions at odds with the team's perceptions when it comes to the organization's actual values. With careful attention to their communication style, though, 15° Founder can avoid this situation.

> It is much easier than leaders may think to find their perceptions at odds with the team's perceptions when it comes to the organization's actual values.

As you grow your organization, you'll want to ensure you've established a culture strong enough to define healthy guardrails for how you and your leaders communicate with your talent. I've had the opportunity to work in companies of all sizes, and on the whole, I've observed three prevailing communication models: exploitative, empowered, and transactional.

To explain these models, I have paired them with films that feature notable leaders and provide memorable visual examples of each one.

## Exploitative communication:
## The case of the Oompa Loompas

Many of us were introduced to Charlie and his chocolate factory as children, either by reading Roald Dahl's novel or through one of the film adaptations, 1971's *Willy Wonka and the Chocolate Factory* or 2005's *Charlie and the Chocolate Factory*. The plot is relatively straightforward: An eccentric chocolatier reopens his chocolate factory and grants access to five lucky children who found golden tickets in their chocolate bars. Plus, there is an even more spectacular prize for one of the winners. When we meet the winners, we find that four of them would, shall we say, do well with some new parenting strategies. And, of course, there's Charlie, who's gracious, kind, and humble and whose family is rich in love but abysmally poor.

Then we meet the Oompa Loompas.

In the 2005 version of the film, Johnny Depp introduces the Oompa Loompas with a flashback to where and how he first met them, then he admits that he began using them exclusively in his factory because they were cheap labor. It should be noted that in the book's first version, there were overt racist elements to the Oompa Loompa character. According to a 2020 *JSTOR Daily* article, those elements were largely removed in republishing the book a decade after the original work (Gershon 2020).

In the 2005 version of *Charlie and the Chocolate Factory*, all of the Oompa Loompas look the same, though their outfits shift in color and style based on their job at a given time. They are effectively an army of miniature beings whose entire purpose is to bring forth whatever new machinations are brewing in the mind of their rather odd employer.

As far as the story (and presumably Willy Wonka) is concerned, they have no goals or desires beyond being faithful servants to the chocolate factory. We are even invited to consider that Willy Wonka had done the Oompa Loompas a great favor by removing them from their native environment and allowing them to work. Perhaps the Oompa Loompas agree, or maybe not. As Willy Wonka's loyal foot soldiers, their opinions seem irrelevant.

This is a scenario in which we see exploitative communication models thrive. There is typically a leader who needs beings to execute their organizational vision. This leader honestly couldn't care less about these beings' hopes and dreams—they simply need them to get to work. From the leader's perspective, these employees are a collective (e.g., the Oompa Loompas) or simply a resource to be deployed as-needed. Using this frame of reference dehumanizes them just enough to enable the leader to think of them as generally interchangeable and individually expendable. They are tools used at the leader's discretion, and in many cases, the leader genuinely believes they are doing the employees a great service.

What makes this communication model exploitative, though, isn't just how the leader thinks of them. Instead, it's the fact that most often, the leader knows these employees are limited in their ability to find another employer to meet their needs. Armed with this insight, the leader engages in a manner that perpetually reminds their employees of their status as *less than*. While images of sweatshops may be the first to come to mind for "exploitation," we may also find pockets of this in many large, seemingly desirable corporations. The key markers here are the leaders' dehumanizing perceptions. Individual interests are unacknowledged or outright discouraged.

Exploitative models thrive with a one-way approach to communication: leaders give orders, employees follow them. This means employees will only engage as instructed, leaving all independent thought for the leader. For this reason, organizations that use this communication model will perform only at the leader's level because the employees have no real voice. As such, Willy Wonka will never be able to create something bigger than he alone can imagine because *he* is his organization's limiting factor.

For 15° Founders, the same is true. An exploitative communication model can quickly turn a leader into the rate-limiting step to the organization's success. As such, I implore you: Do not engage your team like they are your army of Oompa Loompas. Doing so will severely short-circuit all efforts to build a high-performance culture for a diverse team.

> An exploitative communication model
> can quickly turn a leader into the rate-limiting
> step to the organization's success.

## Empowered communication:
## The case of Charlie, leader of the heist

On the far opposite end of the spectrum from Mr. Wonka and the Oompa Loompas is Charlie and his team from *The Italian Job*. Initially released in 1969, the 2003 remake graced us with an almost-too-good-to-be-true leader. In the film, Charlie successfully leads a team of thieves through a heist in Italy. After a plot twist, though, he reassembles the team to execute a dangerous second heist.

While I recognize *The Italian Job* is a movie about a heist—and I, for one, don't condone stealing as a business strategy—Charlie, the leader of this team of bandits, provides an incredible example of empowered communication between a leader and their team. Though he was the group's founder, he relied on each team member's expertise to bring the vision to life. It should also be noted that each team member had a truly unique skill set, with no overlap. This meant there had to be high trust across the team, which Charlie had to model.

It is no coincidence that trust is at the heart of an empowered communication model and a prerequisite to designing a high-belonging culture. Empowered connection happens when trust is implicit in the who, what, when, where, how, and why of a leader's communication. This engagement model communicates to team members that they are cocreators in the organization's journey and, thus, critical to its success. So, it should be no surprise that empowered communication tends to happen in organizational cultures with high levels of belonging. In these environments, opportunities for innovation are boundless because of the combined dedication and brain-power of the 15° Founder and their team. This is an ideal environment for any leader actively building a new venture.

Empowered connection happens when trust is
implicit in the who, what, when, where, how,
and why of a leader's communication.

As we've established, 15° Founders who this communication
model with their teams and foster accepting cultures do *not*
happen by chance and, I believe, are far less common in
today's workplace than they should be. Suppose you, as a
15° Founder, are privileged to have had personal experience
with a high-belonging, empowered communication culture
built for a diverse team. In that case, you are among the few
with a reference point that may be useful in your current
venture. However, suppose you have not experienced this
personally. In that case, you will need to resist any tendency
to mimic what you may have seen in other workplace environments to instead deliberately institute a new communication framework.

By starting with a genuine respect for different backgrounds, lived experiences, expertise, and insights, then
embedding that respect into the organization's core cultural
values, you will have a mechanism to ensure that respect is
foundational to the who, what, when, where, why, and how
of your own communication style.

## Transactional communication:
## The case of Initech

The most prevalent and, I believe, the most problematic communication style we see in workplaces today is the transactional one. There are myriad reasons for this, not the least of
which is a guy named Frederick.

Frederick Winslow Taylor, born in 1856, achieved fame in mechanical engineering because of a 1906 paper demonstrating how to optimize any metal-cutting task (Hounshell 1988). For mechanical engineering at the time, this was a big deal. But as it turned out, that wasn't the only thing that occupied Frederick's time and attention. Management theories for manufacturing were among his other hobbies, and Taylor—now considered one of the first management consultants—published his thoughts in a book entitled *Principles of Scientific Management* (Hounshell 1988).

According to Encyclopedia Britannica, Taylor's views boiled down to the idea that, in manufacturing, the way to increase outputs efficiently is to put the right folks in the right roles, and pay for their performance (Encyclopedia Britannica 2022). His perspective was that management should *not* pay for new ideas or innovations from the workers—only for performance. Leaders were to monitor them closely, measure their output, and reward top performers disproportionately as incentive.

Today, while we may not necessarily see Taylorism in its *purest* form in a corporate setting, I'd argue it's fair to think of this philosophy like crabgrass: You can cut it down, but it never entirely goes away.

When leaders employ a transactional communication model, employees perpetually receive the message they are simply a resource being paid for a job, nothing more, nothing less. It differs from the exploitative model in that this mode of communication anchors on an employee's utility, not their status or class.

The cult classic film *Office Space* serves as a great illustration of this model. The 1999 film is an homage to pre-pandemic corporate America, replete with morning commute traffic, cubicle farms, and, for some, a nagging sense of dissatisfaction with their life choices. In the film, we meet Peter, Michael, and Samir, three Initech employees who are discontent with work. Things get sketchy when their boss, Bill Lumbergh, introduces management consultants to help them improve efficiencies. Add in hypnosis, a perpetually faulty printer, and Milton, and it's easy to see why this film became such a hit.

At its core, though, the film showed us how the seeds of Taylorism can afflict workplaces far beyond the context of manufacturing. In a pivotal scene, Peter, the protagonist, offers a monologue explaining that he is only motivated to work hard enough not to get fired and that any effort beyond that is of no intrinsic value to him. While it may be tempting to dismiss Peter as an extreme case, it's important to note that if a leader communicates as though team engagement is simply a transaction, it will only be a matter of time before those team members respond accordingly.

As stated earlier, of the three, the transactional communication model is the most prevalent in workplaces across the US. As such, it is dangerously easy to mimic. As a 15° Founder, you cannot afford to take the time to build a bombastically diverse team only to communicate with them as though they are coin-operated machines. Doing so runs the severe risk of undermining your team's potential. As a founder of an early-stage company, your team should consist of people you view as cocreators who will execute the company's vision. You cannot engage transactionally with true cocreators.

> You cannot engage transactionally
> with true cocreators.

# The question that lingered

Throughout writing this book, I would often discuss various concepts with family and friends to hear their questions and feedback so that I could refine them from there. While writing this chapter on communication models, a friend asked a question that lingered in my mind for weeks after the discussion.

> *"Can someone use multiple communication models at the same time?"*

Here's why I love that question: I've explained these communication frameworks with movie characters with clear and distinct personas. The 15° Founders, however, are real people, not movie characters. As such, they can oscillate between communication models depending on the setting, the audience, the day, or even their mood. For most leaders, liaising with internal teams will be a continuous journey with many twists and turns. There are no scripts or producers. Instead, the 15° Founder and their team work each day to achieve the mission and delight customers.

It is essential for 15° Founders to remember the need to streamline empowered communications and avoid transactional and exploitative models with your core teams. Now, understand there may be situations wherein a transactional communication model may be appropriate, such as when working with a supplier or vendor. (In case you were wondering, there will not be a justifiable reason for using the exploitative communication model.) Only the empowered model will help to embed the trust required to ensure the team's diverse perspectives are genuinely valued for the blind spots they address.

Success for 15° Founders in internal communications will be driven by awareness and the willingness to course correct—not perfection. Be aware and intentional about empowered optimization with core teams, as this is the only model that, in earnest, can support a high-performing, high-belonging diverse culture.

## Chapter summary

- Communication breathes life into your culture. As such, 15° Founder must be aware of three communication models and be intentional about which one they use at any given time.
    - Exploitative communication (*Willy Wonka*)
    - Empowered communication (*The Italian Job*)
    - Transactional communication (*The Office*)
- The empowered model aligns with a 15° Founder's organization because it requires trust in the diverse skills and experiences needed to drive a nuanced business strategy.
- The 15° Founder may find themselves oscillating between models. Remember, success is driven by awareness and a willingness to course correct.

# BREATHE LIFE INTO YOUR CULTURE THROUGH COMMUNICATION— PART 2

---

Let's reflect back on our fictitious *Top Host* reality competition. Recall that the goal of the show is to be crowned Top Host. To win, we've focused on two guest lists: one consisting of James Beard Award-winning chefs and the other comprised of a seventeen-year-old entrepreneur, a retired three-star general, a TikTok influencer, a mechanical engineer, and your most eccentric cousin.

Let's consider the hosts who need to craft the ultimate experience for these two guest lists. Based on the differences between the experiences they are creating, do you expect them to communicate to their guests in the same manner?

In my experience, these hosts will certainly approach the two groups differently. The 15° Founders are similar in this respect. As discussed in the last chapter, their communication will distinguish them.

That said, even excellent communication cannot rescue a toxic or disingenuous culture. It can, however, ensure the desired culture translates into the organization's brand. That's why using effective communication to propagate the culture internally *and* externally must be a priority for 15° Founders. When this doesn't happen, team members and customers alike can question whether or not your organization is what they thought. To illustrate, I will share two examples of organizations I've encountered that took very different approaches to communications with external customers.

## Example 1: The rate hike

My son was about two years old when he started at a new Spanish immersion preschool. Friends had referred us, and the owner/director was fantastic. She was passionate about sharing the Spanish language with children from all backgrounds. Furthermore, my son started there at the start of the COVID-19 pandemic, and we liked how proactive the school was in its safety protocols. So we joined the school, and my son enjoyed it. Without question, we've had a fabulous experience.

Then, in the summer of 2022, we received a notice that tuition would increase. The increase was substantial, but we weren't surprised given the economic changes between 2019 and 2022. A few weeks later, I learned that two of my son's friends were leaving from their parents. They had traded notes on the school's handling and realized they'd been offered different discounts. Yikes! According to one of the parents, the discrepancy undermined their trust in the school and communicated a lack of transparency—two areas in which no parent wants to have doubts regarding an educational institution.

Now, here we have a preschool navigating the treacherous waters of COVID-19 and certainly needing to adjust support staff and business operations. I suspect they didn't want to increase rates during the height of the pandemic and create even more hardship for frontline parents. So, by the summer of 2022, it's fair to say they absolutely should have increased the rates. The misstep, however, came in the variance between communications.

Granted, the school may have had very valid reasons for offering different retention discounts to different families. However, from the families' perspective, that variance undermined the idea that all children would be treated fairly and equitably in this environment. Though the school never overtly said this, their handling of this situation also didn't overtly *not* say this.

Imagine if this same school had communicated the following to everyone:

*Dear parents,*

*As you've likely guessed from the title of this e-mail, our rates will be increasing as of July 2022. We are excited to use this opportunity to increase salaries for our teachers and staff who have faithfully supported our children these last two years. We are also excited to use these additional funds to provide new playground equipment*

Had we received this note, we would have paid higher tuition *and* felt compelled to donate to a community fund. More importantly, by shifting the focus of the message from the rate increase itself to the need for better overall community support, the preschool would have been able to convey trustworthiness by being transparent about the reason for the rate hike, fairness in access to scholarship funding, and genuine care about the community created by the school staff and families.

As a bonus, they would also have created an opportunity to deepen the sense of belonging in this community with invitations to receive or provide financial assistance. I have to believe these are all precisely the values this language immersion preschool would want affiliated with its brand.

In this case, a simple but essential operational e-mail was a missed opportunity to reinforce brand values. But take note—even missed opportunities communicate something. That's why communication is so critical. As 15° Founders, you are *constantly* communicating. Whether you are intentionally engaging your team, investors, vendors, or none of the above—you are communicating something in all cases. Your communication lives both in positive and negative spaces. It's always on, and as the leader, you cannot turn it off.

So you must always ask yourself: are you communicating what you intend? Is the message you're sending aligned with the culture you want?

## Example 2: A new local Peruvian restaurant

A new restaurant popped up in our town sometime after COVID-19 started. This was notable because I saw several restaurants close their doors during this period, but relatively few new ones opened. I was curious, so a friend and I made plans to check it out. We walked in during a busy Saturday lunch period and were greeted warmly by the host.

"Just so you know," she says, "we're short-staffed, so our service may be a little slow. We appreciate your patience with us."

"Okay," we said. Now, of course, nearly every restaurant operating in June 2022 in our area was short-staffed. Every. Single. One. We knew because they *all* had help wanted signs on the doors, windows, and just about anywhere else they could put them. Plus, service was hit or miss. As such, I was struck when the host and, later, the server made a point to manage our expectations in this manner. Because they did so, we were unbothered by the speed of the service, which, relative to other local restaurants, was on par, if not better. The servers were courteous and helpful. Most importantly, the food was fantastic. It was a delightful lunch, and we both planned to return.

As I thought about this later, I realized how the simple acknowledgment of being short-staffed influenced my perspective of the restaurant. It conveyed to me that this was an organization that takes service and transparency very seriously. Mind you, this wasn't written on a poster or used as a tagline on their logo. I make that distinction because organizations often attempt to spell out who they want you to believe they are, regardless of your experience of them. As we know in life and as this restaurant demonstrated, actions speak louder than words. But note—both actions and words *speak*. More specifically, your actions, inactions, words, and silence communicate who you are as a brand and leader.

> Actions speak louder than words.
> But note—both actions and words *speak*.

I intentionally chose two examples of organizations that needed to communicate an ordinary matter to customers. In both instances, a simple message from each business informed my perspectives on them. Note that the communication wasn't directly from the leaders. That's why it's extremely important your communication as a leader informs your culture and, by consequence, how your employees communicate with external audiences.

Research by Gochhayat, Giri, and Suar studied the role of communication and culture on organizational effectiveness, which can be thought of as a company's ability to reach its goals (Gochhayat, Giri, and Suar 2017). The study was conducted at technical and management institutes across India, designed to look at culture's impact on organizational effectiveness and the impact of communication as a medium between the two. Essentially, the study found that a strong culture did correlate to higher organizational effectiveness. However, communication was a significant mediator here. This means a strong culture enabled better communication, which, in turn, enhanced organizational effectiveness.

*Communication helps the leaders to reach the followers and motivate them for the attainment of the vision, mission and goals of the organization. The vision and mission of an organization may not yield that result if these are not communicated properly within the organization. Stimulating and inspiring communication helps organizational members to realize values and mission statements rather than being compelled to follow them (Gochhayat, Giri, and Suar 2017).*

## Thought exercise

*You are the executive director of a new education sector business that recruits, trains, and places new school-teachers in K-12 schools nationwide. During this past year of operation, your success rate has been 98 percent based on the metrics you've defined—preparation for teaching a given subject, rated as above standard or exceptional by school administration, and, most importantly, staying in a given school for at least three years.*

*You're most proud, however, of the relationship your organization maintains with a growing cadre of phenomenal teachers.*

*Your organizational values are to champion equity, pursue world-class education that meets each child's needs, and recognize and respect the whole person. In the last year, you and your team have noticed a trend. Your alumni are reporting they are burning out from the profession they once loved. They cite myriad reasons, but common themes are low pay, long hours, increasing demands from administrators, and a sense they are unable to teach children the way they've been trained to.*

*Several of your top leaders have come to you with concerns about how the team should train teachers, given the challenges they are likely to face once they enter the profession full-time.*

*What do you communicate to your team, your alums, and your partner schools? How can you do so in a manner that aligns with your organization's values?*

---

*For your team, one approach is to communicate why your core values are so critical in the current environment and, thus, why your organization's mission remains paramount. This can be done in a leadership meeting or via a memo, but the message should be clear: Your work matters now more than ever.*

*For the partner schools, a possible approach would be to communicate that you remain committed to placing world-class teachers in their schools, but you need their true partnership as well. You will need to challenge them to be good stewards of the talent in their midst and remind them that, ultimately, all parties want to enable optimal outcomes for K-12 students. You can also chart a plan to engage thoughtfully with them to identify ways to ensure that teachers receive the best support.*

*Lastly, for your organization's current teachers and alums, one approach could be to communicate that your relationship with them does not end when they complete the program. Your organization will continue to be a resource for them both indirectly by working behind the scenes with partner schools and directly by helping them to find placement with schools that have supportive environments.*

*There will be many ways to communicate thoughtfully with each of your audiences. The critical thing to remember is you must ensure each approach is aligned with your organization's core values and mission and that you follow through with any commitments.*

## Communication in the negative space

In May 2020, George Floyd was barbarically murdered. There had been several murders of unarmed African Americans before George Floyd's. Because of the pandemic, though, people across the globe had fewer mechanisms for averting their eyes from the horror of the incident. Within a few weeks, the Black Lives Matter hashtag started trending, and protests took place across the globe. And then something odd happened.

Corporate statements, both too many and too few.

As an African-American family, there was already a lot to process. These corporate responses gave me a conduit for judging the companies that did and didn't issue them. Why wouldn't every CEO issue a statement acknowledging the heinous series of murders? That said, did any of these companies *mean* any of what had been communicated, or was it all just performative?

Situations like this illustrate the importance of communicating in ways that align with your values and their corresponding behaviors. The worst thing to do is to respond in ways that directly contradict these things. Even though corporate statements about standing with black communities were largely well-intentioned (I believe), once team members, customers, and potential customers recognized a discrepancy between what was said and leaders' actual behaviors, trust was eroded. The biggest challenge many companies faced in the summer of 2020 was that their stated commitment to diversity and anti-racism did not align with previous behaviors exhibited by leadership. As such, many statements seemed disingenuous.

This is when you're supposed to say, "Okay, Michel. But you said communication exists in the positive *and* negative spaces. As such, leaders who neglected to make public statements affirming a stand with the Black Lives Matter movement, in this case, were making a statement too." I hear you.

With that in mind, I had the privilege of chatting with Alida Miranda-Wolff, a passionate diversity, equity, inclusion, and belonging practitioner, author of *Cultures of Belonging*, and founder of Ethos, a consulting firm committed to creating the conditions for everyone to thrive at work. During our time together, she shared a story with me of a client who, she felt, took an approach that aligned well with the values of his organization.

"I noted that he checked in with himself first, and he asked himself what felt true and what felt real," she said. According to Miranda-Wolff, in the all-staff meeting held as a result of Floyd's murder, this CEO affirmed his commitment was to his team, not to how the organization looked to folks externally. He created a safe space for those in his organization to share (or not share) their feelings and shape (or not shape) a public response if the organization chose to do so. He also owned up to the fact his lived experience provided no insights into those of black men in the US.

> When communicating, you must always
> be clear on who your audience is.

I found this story striking because for its account of how this leader communicated both a blind spot in terms of his background and his priority to support his team and not perform for the masses. I do not know if that company ever published a corporate statement or not. Still, I hope that if they did, it was a genuine reflection of their values, behaviors, and culture.

As a 15° Founder, you will most certainly have a stated and overt commitment to diversity, equity, inclusion, and belonging within your organization. That said, it's important to recognize there will be situations that test those tenets. When communicating, you must always be clear on who your audience is. Let your communication be an honest representation of your values and behaviors, not a reflection of what's trending. Ultimately, this clarity of audience and alignment with values will deepen your customers' and team members' trust.

## Chapter summary

- As a 15° Founder, communication is a powerful tool for propagating your culture.
- Communication exists in both positive and negative space—meaning what you say and do not say both matter.
- If your communication contradicts the values and behaviors in your culture, you risk eroding trust.
- When situations test your cultural values, remember to let your communication reflect your true beliefs. If you need to evolve your culture, start that work first before issuing corporate statements.
- When communicating, always be clear on who your audience is.

## CHAPTER 7

# SELF-AWARENESS— YOUR MOST VALUABLE PLAYER

In 2020, my family and I relished any content that allowed an escape from the chaos and mayhem of the world around us. For me, Netflix's ten-part docuseries *The Last Dance* was one of those precious experiences. The series chronicled Michael Jordan and the Chicago Bulls franchise during the 1990s.

Growing up, I was a huge NBA fan. I faithfully watched the regular season and playoffs from a very early age. By twelve, I was such a big fan that I insisted on wearing my Bulls T-shirt to as many sixth-grade basketball practices as our laundry schedule would allow. My coach nicknamed me "Bulls" throughout the season, and every time he said it, I had to suppress an emerging grin while taking his instructions. I'll even go so far as to say if there's ever an episode of *Jeopardy!* with "Chicago Bulls Trivia from the 1990s" as a category, I like my chances. *The Last Dance* allowed me to relive all the best moments of that period.

Back in the day, it wasn't uncommon for marquee players to spend most of their careers with one team. Unlike today, you could buy a jersey with high confidence that it would be relevant throughout that player's career. Today, however, the calculus for these elite athletes is very different. Players and general managers constantly seek to improve the chances of winning a championship (and, of course, the seven-plus-figure contracts that come with it). Math like this requires an accurate and unflinching assessment of the player's statistics (average points, rebounds, assists, etc.) and the holistic value they can create for a team.

The calculus for 15° Founders should be similar. There must be unflinching clarity in your statistics—the skills you have, the skills you lack, your superpowers, your kryptonite. For 15° Founders, "trades" may come as a business strategy pivot, a restructuring of the core team, or even a transition to a new adventure. In each of these situations, though, there is one essential behavior critical to success: self-awareness.

For our purposes, self-awareness refers to the commitment to be unflinchingly honest with oneself about a given situation and one's role in it. According to organizational psychologist Dr. Tasha Eurich, there are two types of self-awareness: internal and external (Eurich 2018). Internal self-awareness is described as how clearly we see our own values, passions, aspirations, reactions, environmental fit, and impact on others. External self-awareness, on the other hand, represents how others view us in terms of these elements. Notably, while 95 percent of people believe they are self-aware, according to one study, only 10 to 15 percent truly are (Eurich 2017).

> Self-awareness refers to the commitment to be
> unflinchingly honest with oneself about
> a given situation and one's role in it.

## Self-awareness—a VC's take

As it turns out, organizational psychologists are not the only ones who recognize the importance of self-awareness in business.

Ethan Austin is the founder of Give Forward, a startup he sold to a company acquired by GoFundMe. Today, Austin runs Outside Venture Capital. I had the privilege of meeting Austin in the fall of 2022 when I asked him to reflect on his entrepreneurial journey.

Becoming an entrepreneur was, in many ways, happenstance for Austin. After college, he and several friends traveled to a few countries before some of them decided to start a hostel. Instead of joining, he decided to go to law school. Once in school, he decided he wasn't very good at it. "I think I can make more money and have more fun building a business," he concluded.

One of the things that jumped out when I met Austin was his striking self-awareness. When I asked him about its role for entrepreneurs like him, he acknowledged it can be a common challenge for many founders. According to Austin, they are uniquely invested in the business unlike anyone else: "As a founder, you're probably the last to see if you're running a zombie company."

As an investor, one of the things Austin looks for in entrepreneurs is whether or not they can self-reflect. This is particularly important to Austin because he now recognizes that teams may become frustrated when leaders fails to acknowledge or brush aside pertinent issues. For early-stage companies in particular, Austin believes the best way to proactively address issues arising from a lack of self-awareness is to codify its principles into company-wide use.

Austin experienced this firsthand as the founder of Give Forward. He recalls having pitched a specific channel strategy to investors and feeling obligated to continue investing in that channel, even when it wasn't generating the desired results. Ultimately, he and the team did successfully pivot to new channels. As Austin reflected on this, he recalled a discussion with those same investors in which they confessed to skepticism about his initial channel strategy. Because they were investing in *him*, the elite athlete in this franchise, they believed he and the team would ultimately figure it out… and they did.

> The best way to proactively address issues that arise from a lack of self-awareness is to codify its principles into company-wide use.

When asked about advice for 15° Founders, Austin offered two pieces.

His first piece of advice focused on the role of communications, which, as we've discussed, is always on and breathes life into culture. According to Austin, investor communications is one area in which many founders struggle. He shared, "Being consistent with investor communications matters [as well as] being truthful […] and showing that vulnerability." As a founder, he admits to being consistent with investor communications when things are great. However, during challenging times, talks may slip from monthly to every other month to quarterly. "Investors don't have magic powers," Austin says, "and can't help if they don't know what's going on."

Austin's second piece of advice for 15° Founders was about differentiation. From his perspective, much of today's technology can be replicated. On the other hand, "culture, values, […] and the way founders lead can set [a company] apart." In other words, it's critically important to get these right. They are the crucial drivers for how the company will execute its strategy. Austin urges founders to think about these things from day one.

Both pieces of advice require 15° Founders to be clear about what's going well with the organization, what isn't going well, what sets it apart, and the role they play in each of these things. In other words, self-awareness is paramount to the success of a 15° Founder—regardless of what team they are on.

## The role of self-awareness in building a team

According to Embroker, a Bay Area-based business insurance company, in 2021, 90 percent of startups failed. Notably, 23 percent of the time, a weak founding team was cited as a cause for failure (Embroker 2023). So, for 15° Founders, self-awareness isn't just about developing a working knowledge of internal and external perceptions regarding one's values and passions. Instead, it also forms the foundation for identifying one's blind spots and covering them with the right team members.

Dr. Scott Nguyen is a fellow at the University of Texas's Energy Institute and the founder of Bodhi, a company devoted to accelerating a more energy-efficient economy. He confesses that becoming an entrepreneur was never his plan. "There's a reason I went and got a PhD in physics!" Dr. Nguyen admitted. He candidly describes his career as a zig-zag from academia toward the solar industry.

Stemming from his academic experiences, Dr. Nguyen admits he has always wanted to ensure employees could grow meaningfully while at Bodhi. With that in mind, Dr. Nguyen is committed to the idea that a growth mindset—the belief that one's abilities can develope through dedication and hard work (Dweck 2006)—is critical to Bodhi's success. As such, he has worked to embed this value within the culture.

For example, Dr. Nguyen recounted interviewing a candidate for a part-time position. After learning about her experience, he challenged her to consider the head of product role—for which she didn't believe she qualified. Ultimately, she not only joined Bodhi as head of product but was also very successful in the role.

"This is an important part of our culture—this combination of looking out for the employee's best interest and embracing professional and personal growth," says Dr. Nguyen.

In our conversation, Dr. Nguyen provided a great example of a leader who understands the power of expanding one's skillset through meaningful learning experiences. As such, he is a vocal advocate for using a growth mindset and has modeled this even in hiring decisions. What is striking here, though, is that the need for this positive mindset is anchored in an awareness of one's need to develop skills in a particular area. For Dr. Nguyen and the team at Bodhi, self-awareness provides critical insights into how to build a team and informs how to build up oneself in the process.

## Coachability and self-awareness

For leaders who are committed to being self-aware, a natural consequence is coachability. According to the Ohio State University Leadership Center, "coachability" refers to the willingness to receive feedback (Flynn 2020). In essence, once you can honestly assess a situation and your role in it, it is much easier to hear about ways to improve outcomes. For 15° Founders, the goal should be to embed self-awareness and coachability into the culture.

Ade Omitowoju, who we met earlier, is an entrepreneur currently serving as a managing director at Black Venture Capital Consortium (BVCC). When asked if he'd ever considered the culture as a factor in investment decisions, he admitted it can be challenging to gauge early on if the company is, say, only two people. However, he does consider how the founder makes decisions, manages stress, and the extent to which they are coachable. Coachability, in fact, was a significant factor. According to Omitowoju, when the founder isn't coachable, it is often a red flag because they may be using people as a means to an end and might not be open to new ideas. "These things manifest themselves as the company gets larger," he added.

To understand if the founder is open to new ideas, as the founder's team gets larger Omitowoju considers its composition. So, while culture can be hard to determine when the company is one to two people, it becomes clear quickly after hiring multiple team members.

When asked for advice for 15° Founders, Omitowoju shared how a founder initially engages the team will set the tone. "If you want to drive excellence and high performance, but you compromise in certain areas, it creates cultural confusion because your leadership ambitions don't match your activity," he says. In other words, a 15° Founder must be acutely aware of the behaviors they are modeling and the behaviors they are communicating as desirable. If there is a mismatch here, the culture will reflect it.

Omitowoju also offered 15° Founders advice for ensuring an empowered communication model is standard operating procedure for the founder and core team. He advises them to get comfortable empowering others to take charge of their functional areas without being overbearing. Micromanagement can often indicate internal insecurity within the company. When building a team, Omitowoju says, the goal is to set a vision that is then communicated: "You don't want to have one monolithic way of doing things, backgrounds, experiences, etc., because it won't position you well for capitalizing on the market opportunities." In other words, a lack of awareness in one's communication model can very much impede 15° Founders and their select team from winning the championship.

Self-awareness is essential for any effective leader, but for 15° Founders, it is imperative. It provides the necessary insights for building a team with the diverse perspectives, skills, and competencies needed to accomplish your organization's mission.

## Chapter summary

- Self-awareness provides 15° Founders with the insight needed to understand their blind spots and what skills are required to address them.
- Self-awareness is essential to ensuring 15° Founders are not unintentionally undermining their culture design efforts.
- Coachability paired with self-awareness enables 15° Founders to maximize their organization's potential.

## CHAPTER 8

# THERE'S NO CHEAT CODE FOR INTEGRITY

In Ghanaian tradition, eight days after a baby is born, the family has a naming ceremony or "Outdooring" (Kudadjia 1997). Back in the day, the Outdooring would always feature someone dipping their finger in water, placing it on the baby's tongue, then dipping their finger in alcohol and putting that on the baby's tongue. The idea behind it is to symbolize the child learning the difference between good and evil, truth and falsehood. The baby then receives prayers and the child's names are shared with those in attendance, after which there is a party.

I learned this from my dad in preparation for the naming ceremony of my first son. While we did a much simpler, Americanized version, I still appreciate the symbolism around building character in a person from infancy.

Call me old fashioned, but I am convinced the main trait distinguishing 15° Founders is their character. While it may seem almost taboo to discuss the importance of a person's character in modern times, it is striking to me that the most salacious headlines about business leaders almost invariably revolve around some indiscretion or dishonesty—both of which become indictments of the person's character.

Before I go too far here, let me acknowledge two things. First, when I refer to a person's character, I am referring to the definition given to me as a child: the things you do, say, and even think when no one is watching. This is derived from the often-quoted passage from the Bible, "For as he thinketh in his heart, so is he" (Proverbs 23:7, KJV).

This leads me to the second point: I was raised in the church—the southern, predominantly African-American, "third place" long before there was Starbucks church. So, my Christian faith and belief system will inform my perspective here. But regardless of your religious affiliation or lack thereof, the importance of character for 15° Founders cannot be overstated.

All one needs to do is check the headlines.

In October 2022, Elon Musk became owner and CEO of Twitter. The headlines that followed this acquisition were as if a sports analyst were running play-by-play commentary for a cringe-worthy athletic debacle. Every decision he made became trending news, and few headlines intimated confidence that Musk was making sound decisions aimed at building a great culture for a diverse team.

Regardless of how you feel about Musk, Twitter, or the acquisition itself, it's noteworthy at the core of this media coverage was whether or not he had the temperament and character to lead a social media company.

I know what you're thinking. "Well, Michel, any random selection of headlines is bound to be based on the writers' biases." I hear you. But here's the thing. In November 2022, I posted a LinkedIn poll to gauge the impact media coverage of the acquisition had on perceptions of the platform. The post went like this:

> *Twitter has been trending a lot lately, but I cannot help but consider that this saga has a very real impact on the lives of very real people. Given this real-time view of the internal "workings" of the company, I also wonder how these events will impact external perceptions. I'd love to get a quick pulse on this with the survey below.*
>
> *Based on recent media about Twitter, is your perception of the company today different from what it was a year ago?*

Thirty-four individuals responded, and the results were as follows:

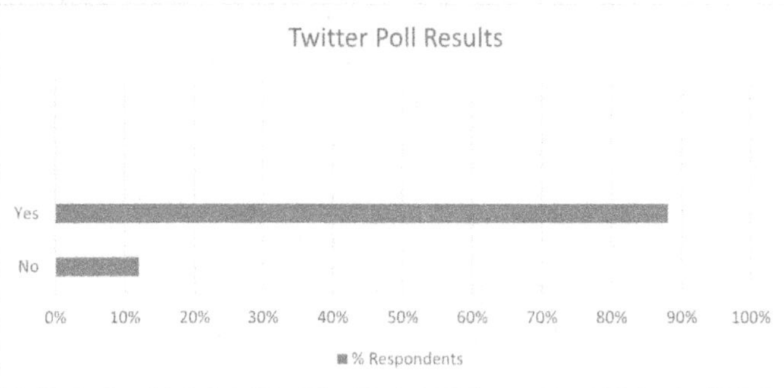


This suggests that—regardless of how one may feel about the media coverage or even Musk himself—merely questioning his motivations for leading Twitter was enough to make some of its users shift their perceptions about the product itself. In essence, the leader's character, as reflected through their actions and inactions, doesn't just matter for their own sake; it matters for how customers and potential customers perceive the brand and products. Character doesn't just matter for its own sake. It matters for the sake of successfully building the business.

> Character doesn't just matter for its own sake.
> It matters for the sake of successfully
> building the business.

At around the same time as the Twitter situation, another major business story was taking place: the collapse of FTX, the cryptocurrency exchange platform. By mid-November, Bloomberg and other major media outlets reported the company had filed for Chapter 11 bankruptcy protection (Hill 2022). Further probing into FTX's financials suggested what I would describe as a glorified Ponzi scheme with a cryptocurrency twist. As headlines swirled, Sam Bankman-Fried reportedly tweeted that he was "… sorry," and "… should have done better." But the apology may have been insufficient for the FTX clients who, according to Reuters, lost at least one billion dollars collectively. As of the writing of this book, this case was still under investigation (Berwick 2022).

I reference the Twitter and FTX stories because, when I stepped back to think about it, every single business scandal I know of—and I mean every single one—can be traced back to the leaders and their character. In my observations, the issue is often one (or more) of four things: dishonesty, greed, sexual indiscretion, or stealing. The list is so short it's almost disappointing.

Listen, as 15° Founders, I need you to hear me on this. Please do *not* find yourself trending on social media over a short and predictable list of indiscretions.

Mindfulness of your character and that of the folks on your team can prevent scandals 99.99 percent of the time. Sure, a few notable business leaders may appear to have "gotten away" with all sorts of things. Nevertheless, understand that for the vast majority of leaders, it will not work out that way and will cost more than you likely want to pay. In a 2012 article, entrepreneur and philanthropist Amy Rees Anderson positions integrity as a prerequisite for trustworthiness (Anderson 2012). As discussed in earlier chapters, trust is critical for designing organizational cultures for diverse teams, and, as a 15° Founder, your character is a crucial differentiator for your organization. It will influence how you build the team, design the culture, communicate, and remain self-aware. Effectively, it drives everything that makes you a 15° Founder.

With that in mind, there are three towering character traits in 15° Founders.

## 1. They are honest.

It's that simple.

For 15° Founders to be 15° Founders, they must have the self-awareness to recognize their blind spots and the willingness to address them. They must also be committed to intentionally building teams around these blind spots, ones that possess as many dimensions of diversity as possible—racial, ethnic, cultural, gender identity, professional experience, socioeconomic background, and so on. To achieve this, 15° Founders must be honest about their shortcomings and be sincere in the desire to do what it takes.

The reality is that you cannot fake a commitment to building a diverse, high-belonging culture. Eventually, a leader's true sentiments will reveal themselves. So, if you consider yourself a 15° Founder but find yourself not fully bought into the commitment to build a truly diverse team, I challenge you to self-reflect and be honest about your journey as a leader.

**2. They are generous.**

By generous, I don't necessarily mean they give all their money to charity, though that is admirable. Here, I am referring to generosity of spirit.

Have you ever noticed that generosity breeds more generosity? According to UC Berkeley's Greater Good Science Center, human beings are wired for generosity, which is associated with improvements in overall health and happiness (Allen 2018). Furthermore, generosity in the workplace is associated with reducing the likelihood of job burnout (Allen 2018). This matters because designing a culture for a diverse team requires giving consideration to differing points of view and giving credit where it is due, among other things. Weaving these traits into the culture will require leaders to model and reward this generosity in each desired area.

**3. They are vigilant about the culture.**

The 15° Founders recognize that culture is living and breathing, thus requiring constant nourishing. It is not something one can set and forget. Even as they employ the support of facilitators, 15° Founders understand the importance of managing the culture like it is precious and fragile. As such, they avoid distractions that undermine their work to build a culture that supercharges the business strategy. They live in a way that honors the organization's values, even when no one is watching.

As an example of a 15° Founder's character traits, I will again look to Paula Sneed's description of how she built and led her team.

When I asked the former executive vice president at Kraft Foods about how she led teams at a Fortune 500, she said she had to intentionally ensure that day-to-day interactions required the team to work together in positive—not competitive—ways. This way, everyone on the team was bought into the success of the whole. This became particularly important when resources had to be distributed across the team and not every leader could receive the same level of investment.

Sneed also indicated that it was essential to periodically bring the team together for shared experiences and ensure there were no "hiders." She needed to hear *everyone's* voice to know how they felt about critical decisions. "I only needed 80 percent agreement, but I had to have 100 percent alignment once the decision was made," she recounted.

Lastly, and arguably most importantly, she would not tolerate leaders who violated the cultural values she'd put in place. To effectively lead, she needed her team leaders to serve as belonging facilitators, which meant they, like her, had to model the culture values.

Her reasoning for the principle was powerful. She didn't just want to hire good people to help her build and manage the organization—that was only part of the story. Sneed was very clear about the fact that she would not always be the leader. She was always conscious of the need to build businesses that would outlast her and could be transitioned to a successor with relative ease. Since she knew she would be invested in the organization's success well beyond her tenure, she was clear about the need to groom great leaders to ensure its future success.

> Always be conscious of the need to build businesses that will outlast you and could be transitioned to a successor with relative ease.

Sneed beautifully demonstrates the character traits of a 15° Founder. She had to be honest in her commitment to intentionally design highly-cooperative cultures by engineering how the teams would work together, and she had to be sure the leaders she brought in were also honest in this commitment. She ensured generosity underpinned the team because, materially, there were times when investments could not be distributed evenly. Lastly, she showed the importance of being vigilant in protecting the culture with a mindset toward ensuring a successful organizational legacy.

In a nutshell, integrity never goes out of style, and for 15° Founders, there's really no way around it. So, like a Ghanaian baby, never forget the difference between good and evil, truth and falsehood. That way, you avoid being in the headlines for the wrong reason.

## Chapter summary

- A 15° Founder's character sets them apart and will be a primary driver for what makes them a 15° Founder.
- Three traits of a 15° Founder are honesty, generosity, and cultural vigilance.

## CHAPTER 9

# COMMENTARY ON REMOTE WORK

I have a confession: I do not enjoy talking on the phone. To be clear, I very much enjoy staying connected to friends and loved ones. (If you're one of those people and happen to be reading this, you know who you are—and thanks for reading this, by the way.) The thing is, if I could choose an option for how to stay connected with someone, it categorically would not be by phone. To meaningfully engage in a phone call, I must ignore the people and events in my physical space. I have always struggled with that trade-off.

My best friend, however, is the diametric opposite of me. I know few people who can better nurture rich relationships without the need for physical proximity. I've known Reese since high school, and I still remember being quietly shocked when I learned she had her own phone line. Now, this was a big deal in the nineties. We all still had landlines, and for most people, that meant there was only one phone number to reach any of the people living in that home. For many teens at the time, this led to a constant negotiation with parents and siblings for phone time. Reese, however, didn't have that issue.

My best friend is a beautiful example of the idea that building and maintaining relationships with people who are not nearby requires intentional effort. To be fair, building relationships while remote isn't necessarily more challenging than building relationships in close proximity. Both require time, effort, and a genuine desire to put in the work. Is it harder to make time for monthly virtual lunch dates with a new colleague based in a different region or to schedule a monthly dinner with a new neighbor? Is it easier to do virtual coffee dates with a distant relative or to make time for actual coffee dates with a partner? The distinction depends on the ability to invest the time, effort, and desire—not the degree of proximity.

Organizations nationwide are in the thick of this very same discussion about building the relationships required for an optimal organizational culture. According to LinkedIn, 98 percent of remote workers would like to continue working remotely in some capacity for the rest of their careers. The top most cited reason? The ability to have a flexible schedule (Haan 2023).

Meanwhile, a March 2023 CNBC article highlighted that many companies are rethinking their remote work policies in favor of more in-office time (Smith 2023). Why the shift? The answer lies in a question that was posed to me during an interview about this book, a question from an entrepreneur who wanted to know if building a high-performing, high-belonging culture for a diverse, remote team was possible. It was a pointed question that cut at the core of what many leaders are grappling with post-COVID. They want to foster collaboration and protect the culture and are rightly concerned about whether or not they can effectively do this in a remote environment.

To answer the question, I first had to acknowledge that organizational cultures built for in-person teams and those made for remote teams will be fundamentally different. For the former, I would expect behaviors, rituals, and shared elements that require face-to-face interactions. I'd expect to see technology-enabled behaviors, rituals, and shared elements in the latter. One isn't fundamentally better or worse than the other. They are simply different.

Many leaders lament remote work as destructive to their organization's culture. However, this often apportions too much blame on the remote engagement model instead of the culture design itself. COVID-19 forced very many organizations into this exact scenario. Not surprisingly, many leaders could not completely redesign their cultures for a remote team. As such, they found themselves floundering while attempting to nurture a remote team using culture norms designed for an in-person team.

Leaders often prefer in-person engagement because of the belief that collaboration is better done in person. In one *SFGate* article, several Bay Area-based executives are cited for their promotion of the need for workers to return to the office, including Sam Altman, CEO of OpenAI, who famously decried the impact of remote work on staff creativity (Bote 2023). I understand why Altman and others believe remote work undermines collaboration—but I challenge the premise.

A culture built for diverse creatives and designed with collaboration as a core value could promote a wide array of behaviors to reflect innovation. Surely, physically leading in-person whiteboarding sessions could be at the top of the list, but intentionally using the vast array of collaboration tools for a given project to ensure all team members contribute their perspectives could be an equally viable approach. Ultimately, it depends on the behaviors the leader recognizes and models. This designation defines mode of engagement (i.e., remote versus hybrid versus in-person), not vice versa.

## The great return to office

A dear family friend—we'll call her Iris—has what I have often thought of as the quintessential "cool job." She works in the media, and as a consequence of her profession, she frequently has the opportunity to engage a wide array of celebrities and public figures. A textbook creative, she's always been very nonplussed about these encounters.

However, when asked about her organization's culture, Iris admits she has never felt the leadership did much to design it intentionally. She offered, "Sometimes we would play a game together in the office to give ourselves a brain break, but that's about it, really." Iris, an African-American woman, admits she never felt her team was "as close as we could have been for a small team of five."

When the pandemic started, they were forced to figure out an entirely new way to produce content. They genuinely believed creative work was best done in person. So, those first few months of her transition to a remote engagement model were hard to watch. Her team had to bring their bulky office desktop computers home to continue creating their content.

With time, they adjusted to the new normal. Two years later, she'd occasionally lament that the executives were anxious for her team and others to return to the office. She hoped these were just rumors, as she had come to like the new approach. She relayed to me, "COVID-19 completely changed how we worked. The requirements of my job were just different."

These changes were permanent for Iris, and returning to the "old way" was nonsensical. Notably, it wasn't just the shift in job specifics that she came to accept. According to Iris, remote work made it "less awkward to be the team we already were." In her esteem, the remote working model better aligned with the culture that existed even before COVID-19. So when the executive leadership eventually informed everyone they would all need to return to the office, Iris was disappointed. Sales were up, and content was being created seamlessly without any of the early pandemic issues. But the executives indicated that while the metrics looked great, they still felt it was better for people to be in the office together.

When I asked what prompted the change, Iris recounted the narrative swirling around the office about the "real reason" for the policy shift. She specified, "Apparently, one of the executives visited one of the offices and saw very few cars in the parking lot and decided this model was not good for the organization."

Was this the true impetus of the executive team's shift or a well-crafted rumor? We'll never know. However, Iris's company is an excellent example of what many leaders are navigating now that COVID-19 has transitioned from pandemic to endemic. Having managed to stay afloat through crisis, they now recognize the reality of the adage, "Culture eats strategy for lunch." As such, they are quite keen to protect and preserve their organizational culture.

The reality is that for many organizations, the in-person engagement model was simply the pre-pandemic default. It was never an intentional aspect of the organization's culture. So, when COVID-19 forced remote work on us, it begged the question of whether or not culturally beneficial behaviors could be demonstrated if team members were remote. For many organizations—and to the surprise of many leaders—the answer to this question was yes.

## One final note

Regardless of the mode of engagement, 15° Founders should recognize there is no replacement for human connection. Digital tools are an aspect of the modern workplace that we certainly cannot do without. But just as watching the World Cup final between France and Argentina on TV is not the same as being in the stadium, we simply cannot duplicate the experience of human connection.

This is when I fully expect someone to say, "Ah, Michel, you are undervaluing the power of augmented reality." I hear you. Call me old-fashioned. I will posit the experience of human connection can never be truly replicated, no matter the technology. As such, I encourage 15° Founders to use their tech to intentionally foster belonging in meaningful ways. When bringing together a diverse group of people, make sure that time spent together is time that thoughtfully reinforces their sense of belonging with the organization. Furthermore, do this in a manner that does not take the uniqueness of genuine human connection for granted.

In other words, make the experience of being in-person an actual shared experience for your organization's diverse team members, not a tick-the-box exercise.

## CHAPTER 10

# CASE STUDY

---

*Author's note: This case study is based on my experiences working with the founders of a US-based tech startup. Names have been changed.*

Shane, the CEO of Bridge Water Tech, is a fantastic guy. But you categorically do not want to go out to dinner with him. The reason? Invariably, a server will bring glasses of water to the table, and at that moment, you will learn all about the water quality in that city. For the rest of the evening, you'll second-guess every sip.

Bridge Water Tech is a startup that provides insights for water utilities to empower them with the visibility and awareness they need to make decisions in the stewardship of Earth's most precious resource—water.

Bridge Water Tech was founded by Shane and his cofounder, Karsyn, in 2018.

The pair had worked together at another company prior. Five years later, Shane approached Karsyn with a new idea. Its approach wasn't fundamentally dissimilar to the premise of Shane's prior startup. Karsyn admitted his first response was, "I don't see an opportunity in water. We don't even pay for it, and I know nothing about the industry." But Karsyn, a self-described "ride or die dude," quickly adds that after some thought, he told Shane, "I'm down. Let's do this and see if someone will buy."

## Early influences

In chatting with Shane and Karsyn, it became apparent they had different but complementary approaches to building a business. Their respective journeys toward entrepreneurship—a descriptor that made both of them recoil—were eerily similar.

Raised in West Africa, Shane's mom was a science teacher, and his dad was an accountant. "My dad probably wouldn't have called himself an entrepreneur, but [after working for a short period in the private sector] he ended up starting his own business," Shane recounts. As it turns out, his dad's closest friends were also business owners. By virtue of being close friends of his dad's, these men had an outsized impact on Shane. "Subconsciously, those were the influences that made [entrepreneurship] possible in my eyes."

Raised in Texas, Karsyn's story isn't that different. Karsyn's parents were both schoolteachers. In the early eighties, Karsyn's parents decided to strike out on their own and start a business. Unable to get a loan from the bank, Karsyn's parents bootstrapped their business and grew it over the years. "So my formative years were them running that company," Karson shares. In reflecting on this, Karsyn indicated the real benefit of his parents running the business for all those years wasn't the financial gain. "I profited from them having the ability to really set their schedule and be in our lives."

After completing his undergraduate degree in West Africa, Shane moved to the UK, where he completed a master's degree and got his first job as an operations engineer for a power plant. While hunting for this job, he had his first entrepreneurial experience. A few friends were trying to build a business that would help organizations with staffing, and Shane created a product his friends could sell—a staffing optimization tool. The tool was designed to show leaders the best resource allocation strategy given their predetermined rules and constraints.

Shane reflected on his journey to Bridge Water Tech, saying, "Essentially, I've done the same thing throughout my career." That first job at a power plant? Shane was the engineer who figured out how much the plant could generate based on various inputs—maintenance schedules, customer power needs, utilization constraints, etc. Bridge Water Tech? Here, Shane's vision was to aggregate data across a city's water distribution system and enable utility operators to make informed, proactive decisions in managing and distributing water to the populace.

Karsyn spent his undergraduate years as a quarterback for a Division I football team. He recounted the team could not realize its potential and lost more games than it won. "The primary issue wasn't a lack of talent. It was a fixed mindset and a poor culture," Karsyn admitted. From this experience, he learned the meaning of perseverance and the importance of a growth mindset and healthy culture.

He would later have this lesson reinforced while sharpening his skills in business development. According to Karsyn, he runs his multimillion-dollar company like a family business because, for him, the business doesn't exist solely to make a profit. It is a mechanism to help team members support their families.

## What's in the water

According to NPR, on January 16, 2016, President Barack Obama declared a state of emergency in Flint, Michigan (Domonoske 2016). The reason was water contamination. It turns out, the city had such high levels of lead that children across the city began showing symptoms of exposure. According to the *Cornell University Chronicle*, as many as 25 percent of children in Flint may have experienced elevated blood lead levels. This is seven times higher than the national average (Dean 2022).

To Shane, the unfortunate part of this is that there are many more Flint, Michigans, than people realize. Beyond water contamination, water scarcity has become a disturbingly expanding global issue. The *Los Angeles Times* reports that the Colorado River's decline is impacting forty million people who live in cities between Denver and Los Angeles and five million acres of farmland that have depended on the river for irrigation (Arellano 2023). Harvard's Graduate School of Arts and Sciences reported that some models project nearly half of US freshwater basins will be unable to meet monthly demand by 2071, due to a combination of climate change and population growth (Wilkerson 2019).

Shane often remarks that facts like these are why friends do not want him to talk about work when out for dinner.

Based on his experiences in the power sector and his recognition of the relationship between power and water trends,

Shane felt the water utilities market was ready for an intuitively designed insights platform for its operators. His vision was to create a program that identified possible issues in the water distribution system, provided insights on those issues, and outlined recommendations for addressing the problems while minimizing the impact on customers (i.e., all of us).

According to Shane, "Bridge Water Tech is an opportunity to do well and do good at the same time."

## Customer value

When asked about their customers, both Karsyn and Shane became very animated. For Karsyn, the customer was the entity that wanted to buy the promise that Bridge Water Tech was selling. As a business development expert, he conceded, "That's just how my mind works." For Shane, the question of Bridge Water Tech's customers was multi-layered. From his vantage point, the immediate customer was the water utility operators, as they were the folks who would use the Bridge Water Tech platform to make more informed decisions about water system management.

The ultimate beneficiaries of the Bridge Water Tech platform, however, are folks who need to be able to access clean water (again, all of us). In truth, this aspect of their value proposition drove Shane's vision for Bridge Water Tech. His goal was to be the guide for the water industry, enabling optimal decision-making. With this in mind, Shane and the Bridge Water Tech team have often repeated the mantra, "When they know better, they'll do better."

# Link core values to customer value

When asked whether he thought Bridge Water Tech's values and culture in the business's very early years, Karsyn admits, "I didn't." Like many early stage founders, Karsyn's focus was strictly on making sure Bridge Water Tech offered a compelling value proposition to water utility operators. As such, the DNA of Bridge Water Tech's culture had Shane's prints all over it and was a direct nod to the idea of being a guide. Expertise with accountability, empathy, and positive persistence were the values Shane and Karsyn agreed upon before bringing others onto the team. Overall, Shane confessed their values were further refined as more folks joined the team which, as of January 2023, consisted of nine people.

Notably, Shane describes Bridge Water Tech's core tenets as a direct reflection of what he felt was critical for doing the work they needed to do. Some of these were natural strengths for him and Karsyn, while others were not. So, he and Karsyn designed the company's core values to reflect what they needed to achieve for their customers.

Beyond this, Karsyn recounts they always knew they wanted a firm comprised of diverse backgrounds. This was something that was never in question. For Karsyn, though, it wasn't just about optimizing for positive business outcomes. He shares, "I wanted a diverse firm to give opportunity to people who are talented [and who may] not get this type of opportunity elsewhere."

For Shane, building a diverse team was an opportunity to recreate something he had done with a prior business, sharing, "My favorite picture is the team in front of the office … [we were] nine people with zero overlap in lived experiences."

## Tie values to behaviors

Positive persistence. That is the behavior that Shane repeatedly refers to when describing what he wanted to model in Bridge Water Tech's culture, both as a value and as a behavior.

Dr. John Umutoni is Bridge Water Tech's lead technical program manager and in-house water industry expert. According to Shane, he is also the most positively persistent person he's met in his career. For Shane, this behavior is a way to resist the temptation to get discouraged or quit when (not if) Bridge Water Tech faces challenges as it continues to iterate and grow. Undoubtedly a result of having built and sold a business before, Shane is well aware the water industry has not yet benefited from the technological innovations we're accustomed to seeing in other spaces. As such, he believes the industry needs a sherpa to lead it into the future at an appropriate pace. He has complete confidence that, with positive persistence, Bridge Water Tech can serve as that guide globally.

## Underscore with Recognition

Shane is known among his friends and family as an undercover writer who enjoys taking seemingly disparate information and distilling it down so that others can consume it in unexpected ways. Of course, the Bridge Water Tech cofounders leveraged this skill to its fullest extent. In particular, they intentionally communicate their values to new team members and acknowledge the value these individuals would themselves bring. Almost every person to join Bridge Water Tech has received the following:

- A note welcoming them to the team.
- Information outlining how to work well with the cofounders and the team at large.
- Clarity on what matters to the company.
- Bridge Water Tech's core values.
- The unique expertise and value the cofounders believe the new person will bring to the team based on what they know

From here, Shane and Karsyn tried to be very intentional about both modeling positive persistence and other behaviors, as well as recognizing then rewarding these behaviors when team members demonstrated them.

## Activate with belonging

The Bridge Water Tech team created some fun shared experiences for this small but mighty, fully remote team of passionate builders. One example is the end-of-year gift box. As a fun twist, the cofounders shipped a gift containing breakfast ingredients, and the team enjoyed a virtual breakfast together.

It's essential to recognize that Shane's experience with his prior startup certainly informed the thoughtfulness around Bridge Water Tech's culture. While Shane had prioritized building a strong culture, Karsyn admits he was more concerned about what he felt was Bridge Water Tech's biggest challenge—sales. Did they, a minority-led SaaS company, fit the image their customers had for a game-changing platform that would use the latest technology to help them make better decisions on water supply and management? Was Bridge Water Tech positioned to truly serve as an innovative leader for the water utility industry?

For Shane, the answer is unequivocally yes. "Water is getting a lot more attention, and the opportunity is to cater to the ecosystem actors that will benefit most from our tools. The need for information, insights, and predictions to improve decision-making [...] will always be necessary, and we will be here to provide that decision-making support with our tools," Shane explains.

As of January 2023, the Bridge Water Tech team was still working toward achieving this vision—and they expect it to be a breakout year thanks to continued positive persistence.

## Reflections

I had the opportunity to discuss with Karsyn his reflections on Bridge Water Tech's journey in early 2023. One of the topics we explored in depth was the prioritization of culture design throughout the company's journey.

"If you were writing a book about marketing, no one would ask if there's a link to business outcomes," Karsyn posits. When discussing culture, however, he admits to being prone to a healthy level of cynicism.

As he reflected on their day-to-day operations, he highlighted specific times when Bridge Water Tech's culture played a pivotal role in business outcomes. The first area was in their ability to recruit world-class talent. "Our culture allowed us to hire amazing folks. It made them give us a chance," Karsyn says. Dr. John Umutoni, industry expert in US water quality, is a great example of this. According to Karsyn, he joined Bridge Water Tech because he liked the culture and felt aligned with the mission, which was a massive win for the company.

Karsyn went on to explain that their culture's impact on business outcomes wasn't limited to hiring. Investors and early customers who came on board with Bridge Water Tech were also attracted by how the company's culture showed up externally. Karsyn shared, "We looked different and sounded different. Our zoom screen looked like the United Nations… and that made a powerful impression, which helped us to attract customers."

Last but not least, Bridge Water Tech's attentiveness to building a culture for a diverse team was directly linked to business outcomes. In fact, it enabled a diversity of thought that allowed for better customer communication. One example was a customer call on the verge of going awry because there was a breakdown in understanding between the customer and one of the team members. It turned out, though, that the company's head of operations happened to be from the same place as the customer. So, she began messaging the team with clear directions for how to best communicate with that specific customer. "She saved that call, and we got the contract," Karsyn recounts.

In all three examples Karsyn shared with me, it was clear that Bridge Water Tech's commitment to designing a culture for a diverse team had become an invaluable strategic asset for achieving their mission.

# TYING IT ALL TOGETHER

———

At the start of this book, you were a judge in a fictitious reality show, *Top Host*, in which contestants across the country competed for the title of the best host and a chance to win a million dollars. In the business setting, 15° Founders are our Top Hosts. While I cannot guarantee a seven-figure bank account, I can say that you stand to see significant benefits from intentionally designing cultures for diverse teams.

As we embark on the next major evolution of the US workforce, the Great Retirement, our labor pool will become increasingly diverse. As such, the first benefit 15° Founders will experience from culture design is an advantage when competing for talent.

A culture designed for a diverse team will fundamentally differ from one that hasn't been created in this manner. The former will recognize that team members are the organization's first customers and will intentionally invite them to belong within the culture.

Your organization's culture will be a critical point of differentiation, one that attracts highly skilled people from diverse backgrounds and compels them to stay and bring their best to the team.

The second benefit of culture design for 15° Founders is being better optimized to achieve their goals. By building leadership teams that buttress the founder's blind spots, a 15° Founder can expand their field of view to include even more innovative ways to reach goals. While team composition cannot guarantee success, it can certainly optimize the business model and create value for customers.

Last but certainly not least, thoughtful culture design enables 15° Founders to achieve their personal goals for their organizations. Since an organization's culture directly reflects the core leadership, culture design gives 15° Founders the ability to be intentional about what they model. Arguably, for most 15° Founders, this will be the genuine desire to attract and retain a high-performing, deliberately diverse team and the willingness to take meaningful steps to make this desire a reality.

Great cultures for diverse teams never just happen. It's not organic. You will not stumble upon it. And it certainly will not sort itself out. As a 15° Founder and culture gardener, you will need to intentionally "plant" values into your organization's culture and then constantly nurture them so they can take root and grow with the organization. As such, one of the first things that will be rooted in these organizations is a commitment to building and supporting truly diverse teams.

Fortunately, you do not actually need to be a world-class dinner host to build better organizations. You simply need to have the mindset of a 15° Founder paired with the culture design toolkit.

# Using the CULTŪRA Framework

*Step 0: Who am I as a leader?*

What are my strengths?
What are my weaknesses?
What are my values, and how do they inform how I lead?


*Step 1: **Customer value***

Who are my customers?
What problem does my organization solve for them?
Given this, what values do I want them to affiliate with my organization's brand?

*Example:*
*I am the founder of Junction, a non-profit with a mission to bring economic development to urban communities and ensure the community's residents prosper. As such, I consider the community residents my primary customers. When they think of my organization, I want them to experience trustworthiness, community pride, and limitless possibilities.*


*Step 2: **Link core values to customer value***

What culture do I need inside my organization to create the brand I want for my customers?
Given that brand, what should my culture values be?

*Example:*
*Junction's vision is to drive community-level change
that can be replicated across the globe. My culture needs
to reflect a genuine respect for those in the community,
as well as the belief the community is itself valuable. I
will need to ensure my employees align with the same
values I want my customers to associate with my brand,
so my core values should include trustworthiness, pride
in the community, and limitless possibilities.*

*Step 3:* **Tie values to behaviors**

What does it mean for the employees in your organization to demonstrate these values?
How will you and your leaders model these behaviors?

*Example:*
*Behaviors that reflect Junction's values*
*Trustworthiness: We create opportunities to educate the
community about policy decisions that impact them,
such as voter education and registration, back-to-school
drives, and college and trade school readiness workshops.*
*Pride: We show up to community events with excellence
and bring positive energy to each one.*
*Limitless possibilities: We create opportunities for community members to cocreate in its evolution, including,
for example, creating a means for community members
to give feedback on architectural renderings of a new
Small Business Resource Center.*

*Step 4:* **Underscore** *with* **Recognition**

How will you as a 15° Founder recognize and reward the behaviors that reflect the organization's values?

*Example:*
*As the leader, I need to set the bar by modeling these behaviors and recognizing when team members do them. I can incentivize these behaviors by speaking openly about them, providing financial awards for outstanding efforts, or even featuring our team members on social media.*


*Step 5:* **Activate** *with belonging*

How will you foster belonging for your diverse team?
Who will serve as the facilitator of your culture?
What rituals and shared elements will you use to cultivate belonging within your organization?

*Example:*
*Early in the creation of Junction, I will ensure team members experience belonging by serving as both the leader and culture facilitator. As the facilitator, I will constantly reach out to team members and make sure these invitations thoughtfully extend into the community we serve. With that in mind, I will craft rituals and shared experiences that reinforce belonging for employees and community members.*

*Sample initiation ritual:*
*—New Team Member Initiation: As part of onboarding, new hires are invited to a small community dinner that culminates in a symbolic handshake with an elder. A local artist is invited to the dinner to capture an image of the handshake, which is then framed and added to a wall in our office space.*

*Sample shared experiences: a community scavenger hunt, picnics at the local park, and hosting an annual street fair for local businesses.*

*Step 6: Reminders on communication and integrity*

In what ways can I ensure my internal and external communications align with my organization's core values and desired behaviors?

*Example:*
*As a leader, I must remember my communication exists in both the positive and negative space. I will need to be mindful that what I say and don't say, do and don't do are in line with our cultural values. So, as an example, I should ensure that, where possible, Junction's vendors are businesses from the community, from team lunches to event spaces.*

*Lastly, I must continuously optimize my "say-do" ratio by ensuring I am who I say I am and do what I say I or my organization will do. There is no workaround for integrity.*

# Chapter summaries

## Chapter 1

- Eighty percent of culture can be attributed to the founder/core leader.
- While culture is often not a priority in new organizations, it absolutely should be!
- Designing cultures for diverse teams is not easy, but the payoff is enormous.
- An organization's culture is a critical driver for its brand. As such, founders should think of their employees as their first customers.
- Founders committed to designing cultures for diverse teams will have a competitive advantage in attracting and retaining talent.

## Chapter 2

- The Great Retirement, accelerated by the COVID-19 pandemic, will bring significant shifts to the US workforce and will require leaders to activate historically underrepresented talent pools.
- Leaders who intentionally build organizational cultures optimized for diverse teams will be better positioned to compete for the best talent.
- Successfully building an organizational culture for a diverse team requires a leader to be very clear on who they are and are not, as well as their blind spots.

- The 15° Founders are leaders who are aware of their blind spots and build teams that balance out those weaknesses.
- Being a 15° Founder will be an uncomfortable but worthwhile journey.

**Chapter 3**

- When designing an organization's culture, 15° Founders must remember their employees are their first customers.
- Your organization's culture is the link between the employee and the customer experiences.
- A high-performing, high-belonging culture built around a diverse team never happens by accident. It results from a leader who has intentionally designed it and embedded diversity as one of its core values.
- The CULTŪRA framework can help 15° Founders navigate the intentional culture design process.

**Chapter 4**

- Belonging can be thought of as an invitation that must be both offered and accepted.
- Belonging can be engineered based on these three principles:
    - Yes, you can design belonging, but only if you mean it… for real.
    - Belonging is cultivated at the micro level, not the macro level.

- A high degree of belonging within an organization, done well, can translate into a high-belonging experience for your customers.
- Within the first principle of belonging, there are four ingredients needed to cultivate belonging within an organization:
  - Leaders
  - Facilitators
  - Shared experiences and elements
  - Rituals

**Chapter 5**

- Communication breathes life into your culture. As such, 15° Founders must be aware of three communication models and be intentional about which one they use at any given time.
  - Exploitative communication (*Willy Wonka*)
  - Empowered communication (*The Italian Job*)
  - Transactional communication (*The Office*)
- The empowered communication model aligns with a 15° Founder's organization because this model requires trust in the diverse skills and experiences needed to drive a nuanced business strategy.
- The 15° Founders may find themselves oscillating between communication models. Remember, success is driven by awareness and a willingness to course correct, not perfection.

**Chapter 6**

- As a 15° Founder, communication is a powerful tool for propagating your culture.
- Communication exists in both positive and negative space—meaning what you say and do not say both matter.
- If your communication contradicts the values and behaviors in your culture, you risk eroding trust.
- When situations test your culture values, remember to let your communication reflect your true values and behaviors. If you need to evolve your culture, start that work first before issuing corporate statements.
- When communicating, always be clear on who your audience is.

**Chapter 7**

- Self-awareness provides 15° Founders with the insights needed to understand their blind spots and what skills are required to address them.
- Self-awareness is essential to ensuring 15° Founders are not unintentionally undermining their culture design efforts.
- Coachability paired with self-awareness enables 15° Founders to maximize their organization's potential.

**Chapter 8**

- A 15° Founder's character sets them apart and will be a primary driver for what makes them a 15° Founder.
- Three traits of a 15° Founder are honesty, generosity, and cultural vigilance.

# ACKNOWLEDGMENTS

First, I thank God this book came to be! This was a faith journey, and what a beautiful gift this journey has been.

Thank you to the Manuscripts team and the Book Creators community: Ty Mall, A. E. Williams, Kenneth W. Cain, Pavita Singh, Assaunté Wilson, Sherman Morrison, Jacques Moolman, Kristy Carter, Nikola Tikoski, Gjorgji Pejkovski, Michelle Pollack, Noah Fenstermacher, Heather Romanowski, Lyn Solares, Michelle Felich, and Eric Koester. You pushed (and, at times, politely dragged) me over the finish line to complete this book, and I am grateful to have been able to do this journey with your unwavering support.

Thank you to the community who have continually encouraged me throughout this process. In particular, thank you to Reza Shirazi and Rachel Wilson for your encouragement and for reading an early version of this book.

Chitra Thankaswamy, you played such a pivotal role in my career and in the creation of this book. I am eternally grateful for you and your mentorship.

Anaezi Modu, you told me I could do this book long before I believed it myself. Thank you for your vision and boundless generosity in sharing your wisdom with me.

Paula Sneed, Ade Omitowoju, Charisse Conanan Johnson, Dr. Scott Nguyen, Ellen Bailey, Ethan Austin, Alida Miranda-Wolff, Emily Achler, Tawana Rivers, Jennifer Fry, Melanie Fabiyi, Wagahta Semere, Jamail Carter—I cannot thank you enough for trusting me with your stories and allowing me to share them in this book.

Last but certainly not least, thank you to my tribe: Kendra, Cassandra, Elias, Noah, and Seyi. I would have never finished this without you checking in daily, sharing ideas and insights, forcing me to take breaks, and reminding me to enjoy the journey.

Elias and Noah, this is your special shout-out. I love you both to the end of the galaxy and back.

Seyi, so much of this book was inspired by the experience of doing life together with you. I thank God daily that I get to do this journey with you. Thank you for literally making sure I ate every day throughout the process of writing this book and for being the best supporter I could ever dream of having. 1434.

# APPENDIX

## Introduction

*First Round Review.* 2014. "80 percent of Your Culture Is Your Founder." April 15, 2014. https://review.firstround.com/80-of-Your-Culture-is-Your-Founder.

NHTSA (National Highway Traffic Safety Administration). 2011. "Blindzone Glare Elimination Mirror Method." Washington, DC: NHTSA. https://www.nhtsa.gov/sites/nhtsa.gov/files/blindzoneglaremirrormethod.pdf.

Parker, Kim and Ruth Igielnik. 2020. "On the Cusp of Adulthood and Facing an Uncertain Future: What We Know About Gen Z So Far." Pew Research Center. May 14, 2020. https://www.pewresearch.org/social-trends/2020/05/14/on-the-cusp-of-adulthood-and-facing-an-uncertain-future-what-we-know-about-gen-z-so-far-2/.

## Chapter 1

Cole, Nicolas. 2018. "The First 5 Priorities for Every Startup Founder." Crunchbase. December 28, 2018.

https://about.crunchbase.com/blog/startup-founder-priorities/.

*First Round Review.* 2014. "80 percent of Your Culture Is Your Founder." April 15, 2014. https://review.firstround.com/80-of-Your-Culture-is-Your-Founder.

Holloway, Nigel and Dan Armstrong. 2020. "The Experience Equation: How Happy Employees and Customers Accelerate Growth." New Jersey: Forbes insights. https://www.salesforce.com/content/dam/web/en_us/www/documents/reports/forbes-insight%20experience-equation%20ofinal-report.pdf.

Longgrear, Judah. 2023. "Practical Solutions to the Top 5 Challenges for Founders in 2023." *Entrepreneur.* February 20, 2023. https://www.entrepreneur.com/growing-a-business/top-challenges-for-founders-in-2023-and-how-to-solve/444403.

Merriam-Webster. 2023. "Culture." Merriam-webster.com. Springfield, MA: Merriam-Webster. https://www.merriam-webster.com/dictionary/culture.

Van Romburgh, Marlize and Gené Teare. 2021. "Funding to Black Startup Founders Quadrupled in Past Year, But Remains Elusive." Crunchbase. July 13, 2021. https://news.crunchbase.com/venture/something-ventured-funding-to-black-startup-founders-quadrupled-in-past-year-but-remains-elusive/.

Yohn, Denise Lee. 2018. *Fusion: How Integrating Brand and Culture Powers the World's Greatest Companies.* Boston: Nicholas Brealey Publishing.


## Chapter 2


Dimock, Michael. 2019. "Defining Generations: Where Millennials End and Generation Z Begins." Pew Research Center. January 17, 2019. https://www.pewresearch.org/short-reads/2019/01/17/where-millennials-end-and-generation-z-begins/.

Fry, Richard. 2019. "Baby Boomers are staying in the labor force at rates not seen in generations for people their age." Pew Research Center. July 24, 2019. https://www.pewresearch.org/short-reads/2019/07/24/baby-boomers-us-labor-force/.

Parker, Kim and Ruth Igielnik. 2020. "On the Cusp of Adulthood and Facing an Uncertain Future: What We Know about Gen Z so Far." Pew Research Center. May 14, 2020. https://www.pewresearch.org/social-trends/2020/05/14/on-the-cusp-of-adulthood-and-facing-an-uncertain-future-what-we-know-about-gen-z-so-far-2/.

Penn, Rick and Eric Nezamis. 2022. "Job openings and quits reach record highs in 2021, layoffs and discharges fall to record lows." *Monthly Labor Review.* June 2022. https://doi.org/10.21916/mlr.2022.17.

Strack, Rainer. 2014. "The workforce crisis of 2030—and how to start solving it now." Filmed October 2014 in Berlin, Germany. TED video, 12:38. https://www.ted.com/talks/rainer_strack_the_workforce_crisis_of_2030_and_how_to_start_solving_it_now/transcript.

Tanzi, Alexandre. 2022. "'Great Retirement' in US Is Driven by Older Female Baby Boomers." *Bloomberg.* January 11, 2022. https://www.bloomberg.com/news/articles/2022-01-11/great-retirement-in-u-s-is-driven-by-older-female-baby-boomers.

Terrazas, Aaron and Richard Johnson. 2022. "Who Cares about Diversity, Equity and Inclusion?" Glassdoor Economic Research. November 29, 2022. https://www.glassdoor.com/research/who-cares-about-diversity-equity-and-inclusion/.

Yuen, Meaghan. 2021. "Resident Population in the United States in 2023, by Generation." Insider Intelligence. December 14, 2021. https://www.insiderintelligence.com/charts/united-states-population-by-generation/.

**Chapter 3**

Diamandis, Peter. n.d. "Build a Massive Transformative Purpose."
Accessed July 4, 2023. http://www.diamandis.com.

Edmondson, Amy and Mark Mortensen. 2021. "What Psychological Safety Looks Like in a Hybrid Workplace." *Harvard
Business Review.* April 19, 2021. https://hbr.org/2021/04/what-
psychological-safety-looks-like-in-a-hybrid-workplace.

*Harvard Business Review.* n.d. "Harvard Business Publishing."
Accessed November 17, 2022. https://hbr.org/about-hbp.

HBS Working Knowledge. 2018. "Make Your Employees Feel Psy-
chologically Safe." *Forbes.* November 29, 2018.
https://www.forbes.com/sites/hbsworkingknowledge/2018/11/29/
make-your-employees-feel-psychologically-safe/.

Holloway, Nigel and Dan Armstrong. 2020. *The Experience Equation:
How Happy Employees and Customers Accelerate Growth.* New
Jersey: Forbes insights. https://www.salesforce.com/content/
dam/web/en_us/www/documents/reports/forbes-insight%20
experience-equation%20final-report.pdf.

Mahoney, Kevin. 2023. Latin-dictionary.com. Bellingham, WA:
Self Published. https://latin-dictionary.net/definition/15107/
cultura-culturae.

Martin, Murilee. 2017. "50 Years Ago Today, Sweden Switched from
Driving on the Left to Driving on the Right." *Autoweek.* September 3, 2017. https://www.autoweek.com/car-life/a1829546/
50-years-ago-today-sweden-switched-driving-right-driving-
left/.

*Merriam-Webster.* 2023. Merriam-webster.com. Springfield,
MA: Merriam-Webster. https://www.merriam-webster.com/
dictionary/belonging.

Moore, Karl. 2012. "Employees First, Customers Second: Why It
Really Works in the Market." *Forbes.* May 14, 2012.

https://www.forbes.com/sites/karlmoore/2012/05/14/employees-first-customers-second-why-it-really-works-in-the-market/.

Next Street. 2022. "About Us: Our Values." Accessed October 16, 2022. https://nextstreet.com/our-values/.

Savage, Maddie. 2018. "A 'thrilling' mission to get the Swedish to change overnight." *BBC*. April 17, 2018. https://www.bbc.com/worklife/article/20180417-a-thrilling-mission-to-get-the-swedish-to-change-overnight.

Sinek, Simon. 2009. "How Great Leaders Inspire Action." Filmed September 2009 in Puget Sound, WA. TED video, 17:48. https://www.ted.com/talks/simon_sinek_how_great_leaders_inspire_action.

Solis, Brian. 2021. "Here's What Happens When You Focus on Employees to Better Serve Your Customers—Sponsor Content from Salesforce." *Harvard Business Review*. August 2, 2021. https://hbr.org/sponsored/2021/08/heres-what-happens-when-you-focus-on-employees-to-better-serve-your-customers.

World Population Review. 2022. "Countries That Drive on the Left 2023." Accessed November 20, 2022. https://worldpopulationreview.com/country-rankings/countries-that-drive-on-the-left.

## Chapter 4

Ali. 2016. "The Divine Women of Delta Sigma Theta." The Shadow League. January 13, 2016. https://theshadowleague.com/the-divine-women-of-delta-sigma-theta/.

BLCK VC. 2022. "Home." Accessed October 31, 2022. https://www.blckvc.org/.

Brown, Brené. 2018. *Dare to Lead: Brave Work. Tough Conversations. Whole Hearts*. London, England: Vermilion.

Delta Sigma Theta Sorority Inc. 2022. "Home." Accessed November 1, 2022. https://www.deltasigmatheta.org/.

Gonzales, Matt. 2022. "Why Belonging Matters." Society of Human Resource Management. October 15, 2022. https://www.shrm.org/hr-today/news/all-things-work/pages/why-belonging-matters.aspx.

Han, Sheon. 2021. "You Can Only Maintain So Many Close Friendships." *The Atlantic.* May 20, 2021. https://www.theatlantic.com/family/archive/2021/05/robin-dunbar-explains-circles-friendship-dunbars-number/618931/.

National Pan-Hellenic Council. 2022. "Home." Accessed November 1, 2022. https://www.nphchq.com/.

Princeton University. 2022. "Facts and Figures." Accessed November 1, 2022. https://www.princeton.edu/meet-princeton/facts-figures.

Princeton University. 2022. "The P-Rade." Accessed November 1, 2022. https://princetoniana.princeton.edu/traditions/reunions/p-rade.

US Census Bureau. n.d. "Quick Facts." Accessed September 27, 2022. https://www.census.gov/quickfacts/fact/table/US/PST045221.

US Equal Employment Opportunity Commission. n.d. "Diversity in High Tech." Accessed September 27, 2022. www.eeoc.gov/special-report/diversity-high-tech.

## Chapter 5

Encyclopedia Britannica, Inc. 2022. "Taylorism." britannica.com. Accessed June 28, 2022. https://www.britannica.com/science/Taylorism.

Gershon, Livia. 2020. "Roald Dahl's Anti-Black Racism." *JSTOR Daily.* December 10, 2020. https://daily.jstor.org/roald-dahls-anti-black-racism/.

Hounshell, David A. 1988. "The Same Old Principles in the New
    Manufacturing." *Harvard Business Review.* November 1988.
    https://hbr.org/1988/11/the-same-old-principles-in-the-new-
    manufacturing.
Sull, Donald, Stefano Turconi, and Charles Sull. 2020. "When It
    Comes to Culture, Does Your Company Walk the Talk?" *MIT
    Sloan Management Review.* July 21, 2020.
    https://sloanreview.mit.edu/article/when-it-comes-to-culture-
    does-your-company-walk-the-talk/.

## Chapter 6

Gochhayat, Jyotiranjan, Vijai Giri, and Damodar Suar. 2017. "Influ-
    ence of Organizational Culture on Organizational Effective-
    ness: The Mediating Role of Organizational Communication."
    *Global Business Review* 18, no. 3 (April): 691-702. SAGE Pub-
    lications. April 2017. https://doi.org/10.1177/0972150917692185.

## Chapter 7

Dweck, C. S. 2006. *Mindset: The New Psychology of Success.* New
    York: Random House.
Embroker. 2023. "106 Must-Know Startup Statistics for 2023." 2023.
    August 2, 2023. embroker.com/blog/startup-statistics.
Eurich, Tasha. 2017. "Increase your self-awareness with one simple
    fix." Filmed November 2017 in Denver, Colorado. TED video,
    17:17. https://www.ted.com/talks/tasha_eurich_increase_your_
    self_awareness_with_one_simple_fix.
Eurich, Tasha. 2018. "What Self-Awareness Really Is (and How to
    Cultivate It)." *Harvard Business Review.* January 4, 2018.

https://hbr.org/2018/01/what-self-awareness-really-is-and-how-to-cultivate-it.

Flynn, Beth. 2020. "Strive to be Self-Aware and Coachable." *OSU Leadership Center* (blog), Ohio State University. May 19, 2020. https://leadershipcenter.osu.edu/blog/tue-05192020-1219pm/strive-be-self-aware-and-coachable.

## Chapter 8

Allen, Summer. 2018. "The Science of Generosity." White paper prepared for John Templeton Foundation by Greater Good Science Center at University of California Berkeley. May 2018. https://ggsc.berkeley.edu/images/uploads/GGSC-JTF_White_Paper-Generosity-FINAL.pdf.

Anderson, Amy Rees. 2012. "Success Will Come and Go, But Integrity Is Forever." *Forbes.* November 28, 2012. https://www.forbes.com/sites/amyanderson/2012/11/28/success-will-come-and-go-but-integrity-is-forever/.

Berwick, Angus. 2022. "Exclusive: At least $1 billion of client funds missing at failed crypto firm FTX." *Reuters.* November 13, 2022. https://www.reuters.com/markets/currencies/exclusive-least-1-billion-client-funds-missing-failed-crypto-firm-ftx-sources-2022-11-12/.

Hill, Jeremy. 2022. "Bankman-Fried Resigns From FTX, Puts Empire in Bankruptcy." *Bloomberg.* November 11, 2022. https://www.bloomberg.com/news/articles/2022-11-11/ftx-com-goes-bankrupt-in-stunning-reversal-for-crypto-exchange.

Kudadjia, Joshua. 1997. "Integrating Indigenous African Worship and Customs with Christian Worship and Practice: An Illustration with the Outdooring and Naming Ceremony of a Baby Among the Ada of Ghana." Paper presented at the Tenth

Oxford Institute of Methodist Theological Studies, Oxford,
August 1997.

**Chapter 9**

Bote, Joshua. 2023. "OpenAI CEO Sam Altman says remote work
was a big mistake for tech." *SFGate.* May 8, 2023.
https://www.sfgate.com/tech/article/openai-ceo-altman-calls-
remote-work-huge-mistake-18086265.php.

Haan, Kathy. 2023. "Remote Work Statistics and Trends in 2023."
*Forbes.* June 12, 2023. https://www.forbes.com/advisor/business/
remote-work-statistics/.

Smith, Morgan. 2023. "CEOs are quietly backtracking on remote
work—and more companies could follow." *CNBC.* March 30,
2023.
https://www-cnbc-com.cdn.ampproject.org/c/s/www.cnbc.
com/amp/2023/03/30/more-companies-could-increase-rto-
requirements-soon.html.

**Chapter 10**

Arellano, Gustavo. 2023. "Colorado River in Crisis: Part 1: A Dying River."
*Los Angeles Times.* January 6, 2023. https://www.latimes.com/
environment/story/colorado-river-in-crisis.

Dean, James. 2022. "Water crisis increased Flint children's lead
exposure." *Cornell Chronicle.* January 11, 2022.
https://news.cornell.edu/stories/2022/01/water-crisis-increased-
flint-childrens-lead-exposure.

Domonoske, Camila. 2016. "Obama Declares State of Emergency
over Flint's Contaminated Water." *NPR.* January 16, 2016.

https://www.npr.org/sections/thetwo-way/2016/01/16/
463319454/obama-declares-state-of-emergency-over-flints-
contaminated-water.

Wilkerson, Jordan. 2019. "Future Widespread Water Shortage Likely in US." Harvard University. March 20, 2019.
https://sitn.hms.harvard.edu/flash/2019/widespread-water-
shortage-likely-in-u-s-caused-by-population-growth-and-
climate-change/.

www.ingramcontent.com/pod-product-compliance
Lightning Source LLC
Chambersburg PA
CBHW071327140726
47996CB00005B/1858